C000186139

PABLO'S TRAVELS

Also by Pablo Mason

PABLO'S WAR

PABLO'S TRAVELS

SQUADRON LEADER PABLO MASON

with Kim Bartlett

LITTLE, BROWN AND COMPANY

A *Little, Brown* Book

First published in Great Britain in 1996
by Little, Brown and Company

Copyright © Pablo Mason 1996

The moral right of the author has been asserted.

A CIP catalogue record for this book
is available from the British Library.

ISBN 0 316 91400 2

Typeset by Palimpsest Book Production Limited,
Polmont, Stirlingshire
Printed and bound in Great Britain by
Clays Ltd, St Ives plc.

Little, Brown and Company (UK)
Brettenham House
Lancaster Place
London WC2E 7EN

Contents

1

Early Days

It is almost exactly thirty years to the day since I made my first real commitment to the Royal Air Force. But before I was even knee high to a grasshopper I had always known that it was my destiny to become a pilot.

My father regularly took me on days out to airfields around our home in Birmingham, which have long since become housing estates or endless acres of wheat and oilseed rape. We went to Gaydon, which is now a car testing track, and to Castle Bromwich, now a sprawling housing estate which itself faces demolition. There was Elmdon, now Birmingham International Airport, and Bagginton, now Coventry Airport. But it's still the old aerodrome to me with its name written fifties' style on one of the hangar's corrugated tin roofs just to make sure that aircraft without a radio would know where they were. Of course, the state-of-the-art control tower sits across the other side of the airfield ready to be brought into operation. It will launch that airport, screaming, into the latter days of the twentieth century but it will also put to rest a past that still holds so many wonderful memories for me.

Then there were the airshows in the days when the new modern Lightning fighter or the more established Hawker Hunter would roar into supersonic flight over an enthralled crowd. I remember clearly how no one, including myself, turned a hair as these beautiful death machines roared off the runway and overhead with a rush of air followed by a horrendous crack as the soundwave hit their ears. To this day I can guarantee that they did not turn cows' milk sour or break every window in the surrounding villages.

Of course, those were the days of national pride when children's atlases were coloured pink to display the many colonies controlled by this country. To most of us then it seemed the sun would never go down on the British Empire. It was a time when we were still smarting from the Second World War, but this country had proved once more it was a world-beating power and it seemed important to fly the flag. It was not merely jingoistic arrogance, instead it was a genuine belief and confidence in what this small nation was capable of achieving.

At just fourteen years old I gave little thought to the future. While I don't blame my parents for any lack of encouragement on their part, it was simply expected that I should follow in my father's footsteps and eventually take over the family firm as a builder. The very notion that I should take up a career as a pilot was far removed from any aspirations that the Mason parents held for the eldest of their six children. But I could never forget my memories of Cousin Dennis. I actually never met him, but that didn't seem to matter; after all he was the family hero and, therefore, common property to us all.

He had been a young man, typical of all young men in 1940, who had been called out of obscurity to become one of Winston Churchill's few. He had won distinction as a Battle of Britain fighter pilot, and at the end of the war he slipped back into that same obscurity as an ordinary insurance salesman. Although I never knew him I was often told by proud aunts and uncles just how much I looked like him. And it all became part of the destiny I had already set for myself. But when my time came to embark on that course, it happened with such an astonishing lack of ceremony that I still cannot believe how it happened.

It was a Tuesday night in the autumn of 1964 as I rushed home from school to change into my glad rags for an evening's ten-pin bowling with my two best pals, Bob Weston and Graham Andrew. I can clearly recall how smart I felt in my new suede jacket – a birthday present from Mum and Dad. But I can also remember the pubescent spots, greasy hair (in the days when I had hair!) and confusion about girls, who were no longer revolting creatures best to be avoided at all times.

We used up an entire week's pocket money in that evening. Ten-pin bowling was the latest teen craze and it was all we ever wanted to do. The bus home was crowded that night with young lads full of talk about the girls they had seen that night and fancied. Inevitably we ended up getting off at the wrong stop – or was it the right stop? In fact it was two stops before the one for home and it was right outside the headquarters of 165 Squadron Air Training Corps. As we started to walk towards home, grumbling about the fact that we'd stupidly added a good three-quarters of a mile to our journey on foot, we spotted two very smart young men perhaps only a year or two older than ourselves walking towards us. They were dressed in full Air Force airman's uniforms and they walked straight past us, through a gap in the hedge before disappearing inside the air cadet headquarters.

Spontaneity took over – I think in fact it was Graham's suggestion – and we followed them, not terribly confidently, into a large drill hall. The floor was concrete and everyone, apart from the three of us, was clumping around in mirror-finished, steel-heeled, hobnailed boots and wearing very smart uniforms. We were noticed by the corporal who stood at one end of the room. He could only have been sixteen or seventeen years old but he took one look at me and bellowed to me to grab a broom and start sweeping.

His uniform and his stature put the fear of whatever into me and so I picked up that broom and started sweeping for all I was worth. I wasn't even sure where to start because the place was already immaculate. The floor was painted bright red and there was a pot-bellied stove in the centre towards one end of the room which was black and shiny. There was no way you could have lit a fire in it because the inside gleamed as brightly as the outside. All the windows to the hall were crystal clear and the brass fittings shone. Even at my tender age, I could recognise that the whole place lent itself to the old days of 'if it moves salute it and if it doesn't paint it'.

As I swept I glanced through the window out onto the floodlit parade ground and saw three cadets looking just as smart as the ones inside the hall. But these were clearly on some form of jankers. There was a sergeant bellowing at them; I couldn't hear what he was saying, but as he barked at them he walked around them and they did not move an inch. Each of them was holding what I subsequently found out to be a Lee Enfield 303 rifle – a very heavy piece of kit, at arm's length. I suffered that particular form of punishment on a number of occasions during my early days as a cadet and the pain in the arms is quite excruciating. I'd never seen anything like this before yet almost instantly I became magnetically attracted to the order that a military regime dictated.

4

I suppose air cadet life in my younger days must have been something like an old-fashioned public school which, on occasion, could be brutal. The boys could be inhuman towards each other and the non-commissioned officers, barely a couple of years older than us, always demanded 100 per cent effort. It always seemed strange to me that somehow we never quite managed to produce that 100 per cent! Yet there were occasions when, perhaps on a route march exercise when life really was getting too difficult, the sergeant would walk up and grab your kit bag and carry it along with his own. It wasn't a macho thing to do but it made us all realise that he actually cared about the welfare of the younger boys in his charge. What's more, if ever you made a gesture of thanks for such a kindness, it would be shrugged off with a comment about how he didn't want to see the service rucksack get dirty if you dropped it on the ground.

Back to that very first day, it transpired that the corporal who had ordered me to grab a broom and start sweeping was called Mick Richards. We became close friends as we advanced through the ranks together in the air cadet movement. After he left the air cadets he got a job as an office manager at the Co-op. But he also became a confirmed pacifist. From that time he would have no truck with the military and developed intense views about how even the cadet movement instilled all the wrong values into the youth of this country.

I met him some ten years after our first encounter at 165 Squadron. I was already heavily into my basic flying training as a fledgling pilot officer. It was a chance meeting in a Birmingham pub, but when Mick discovered what I was doing for a living he promptly picked up his drink and turned his back on me. I've never seen him since. But at our very first meeting I suppose an hour or so had passed since I'd begun sweeping when he came up to me again saying, 'I'm sorry, but I don't know your name.' I promptly told him and he checked through the list of names on a clipboard in front of him before asking, 'Why aren't you on my list?'

Of course, I explained that I'd just walked through the door only an hour earlier in order to join the air cadets. Typical of an NCO, there was no offer of an apology on his part and I soon learned the golden rule myself: 'You don't apologise and you don't make mistakes'. Anyhow, I was sent along for an interview with one of the air cadet officers; I filled in the forms and I joined. So did Graham and Bob and we all became very loyal members of the air cadets in a very short time.

From the outset I think we were quite different from the boys our own squadron had been used to. First of all, most of the cadets were from secondary modern schools and we were the only three from the local grammar school. Certainly we were greeted with some degree of suspicion by the other cadets.

In brief terms, the air cadet structure mirrors much of that of the Royal Air Force. There are several grades to be attained as a cadet, starting off with first class; how to salute, how to march and the basic parts of a rifle. This goes on to leading cadet where you learn a bit about aeroplanes and the control surfaces that manoeuvre them around the sky. Then you advance to senior cadet picking up a few more details about the principles of flight in a bit more depth and then on to staff cadet. Of course, at any stage you can be promoted from corporal to sergeant, flight sergeant and warrant officer.

Membership of the cadets in those days was certainly

quite a commitment. We used to parade on two nights a week on Tuesdays and Thursdays from 7.30 to 9.30 p.m. and all morning on a Sunday when, if the weather was fine, we'd be out on the parade ground doing drill. Those three periods a week accounted for a considerable chunk of our lives and there were always the hefty duties that crept in, the cleaning, the drilling and the inspections.

The squadron had quite a healthy shooting team sponsored by the local Dunlop tyre factory. In a very short time Bob and I were selected to join the team and we did reasonably well. Graham went along for a couple of trials but it was decided at a very early stage that he couldn't have hit a barn door at three paces . . .

At the end of that first day I felt very excited by what the future had to offer. I'd been interviewed by a young pilot officer in his early twenties called David Lemm. There was something about his uniform that didn't seem quite right to me. It was incomplete, and it didn't take me long to realise that there were no pilot's wings stitched over his left breast pocket. But he explained to me in round terms what the air cadet movement was all about. It encouraged any young man with a desire to take up a career in the Royal Air Force.

I was probably a bit of a rarity, not least for my grammar school education. The majority of the cadets were Birmingham city centre boys from local schools and with a solid working-class background. It meant the squadron was more aligned to providing airman recruits to the technical trades. While I saw an exciting prospect for adventure and travel with the air cadets, I now realise that David Lemm saw the potential in me to become a Royal Air Force pilot. By 9.30 that evening my brain was buzzing with the thought of all those new opportunities that had suddenly opened up to me.

I can remember how Sergeant Jim Beddows came up to me and asked if I could handle a rifle. I immediately said I could even though I had never handled one in my life. In fact the closest I had ever been to a rifle was that evening as I watched the three cadets holding their Lee Enfields at arm's length. By Thursday of that same week there I was, a member of the squadron shooting team practising for a competition. Bob and Graham were asked the same question. Following my lead they had also said they could handle a rifle. I think the assumption had been made that we were grammar school boys and would therefore know all about 'huntin' shootin' and fishin''. Needless to say, nothing could have been further from the truth. But Bob turned out to be a natural with a gun and he always beat me by two or three points in every competition we entered. Right from the very start he and I were always in the top five of the ten-man team. I've still got my shooting medals from all those years ago and they mean more to me than the ones I received from the Gulf War.

I got home at about 10 o'clock that evening and my mum was very upset. She'd had my tea on the table for three hours having expected me home from ten pin bowling at 7.30p.m. Naturally enough, I couldn't understand what all the fuss was about. I tried my best to explain just how important that evening had been and how it was going to open up a whole new world to me. On Thursday I would be shooting; I'd soon be going gliding and flying aircraft. It was just fantastic. My father was less impressed. After all, I'd tried scouting before and, as he pointed out, no sooner had he forked out for a uniform than my interest waned. His comments were predictably dismissive: 'Think

8

yourself lucky lad, if you'd been another five minutes your tea would have been in the bin and my hand would be on your backside.'

I went to bed that night but I didn't sleep much. I *was* going to be a pilot in the Royal Air Force. My parents hadn't realised it yet, but this was only the start . . .

As a family we lived in a large house in Castle Bromwich, then merely a village on the outskirts of Birmingham. There were six children and we all seemed to get on in our own different ways. Dad had a successful building business then and it always seemed to take up most of his time. But Mum was very definitely a family mum.

As far as parental control goes I think my folks were extremely liberal, even by modern-day standards. Our house was a meeting place for most of the neighbourhood kids and it was where we always met to plan what we were going to do together. I certainly enjoyed being the centre of attention as the leader of the pack, and our house was the perfect gang headquarters. At the side was a large yard where Dad used to keep various bits of his building paraphernalia. Inevitably there was always a pile of sand and pieces of timber and scaffolding lying there ready for the next time they may be needed on some building site or other. But to us it was an adventure playground; probably before such things had even been dreamt of as a way of containing youngsters.

Dad did look after us all in his own way. He has never been a terribly emotional sort of man, or certainly not in a physical and obvious way. He's never been the sort of guy to want to give you a big hug or say 'I love you' or anything like that. He just was never very demonstrative with any of us – unless we were heading for a good hiding for some misdemeanour or other.

9

I can recall, when I was a very young child, my brother, Ian, and I tried to make a swing in the garden to play on. It wasn't a brilliant effort but we could manage with the finished product. It was a summer evening but we were still expected to be in bed by the time Dad came home from work, light or not. When he was working hard during those long summer days he really did not want to be bothered with us too much. But next morning when we got up, I can remember looking out of my bedroom window into the garden to see that, not only had our makeshift attempt at a swing had been pulled down, but in its place was a perfect wooden-seated affair properly tied up to a branch of the tree. But it didn't end there. Higher up in the old apple tree in our garden was the most perfectly constructed tree house that we could have entertained a street full of kids in. Dad was off to work again and the last thing he would have welcomed from any of us was a hug or kiss for what he had done. It was just his way of reminding us that he loved us all and he expected nothing more by way of a thank you than that we enjoyed what he had built for us.

In that backyard at Castle Bromwich, we would often have one of Dad's pensioned-off work vans. It had prob- ably started out its life as the baker's van and then gone on to mid-life as a builder's van until it could take no more of the loads and unrelenting demands placed upon it. But that battered old van ended its life as a submarine or an airliner or even a jet fighter plane.

As I grew older I got into the idea of preserving these vehicles and in fact one old car, a Sunbeam Talbot, arrived in our yard because its engine had finally given up and seized completely. But it saw plenty more of life after Ian and I spent weeks tinkering with it. And with the help of our Uncle Roy, a professional mechanic, as well as a fair bit of luck, we actually got the thing going. I can still recall standing back as this old thing belched and spluttered back into life with a huge cloud of smoke and applause from the assembled crowd of kids.

One of the focal points of my year with the air cadets was the seven days I got to spend on a real RAF station. During those seven days we entered drill and shooting competitions. But the very best of all was the thrill of actually being allowed to go flying. We lived as proper airmen during that blissful week. We took our meals in the airmen's mess and lived in one of their quarters.

I dare say things have changed a bit since those days and I expect the youngsters who go away on summer camp now don't even have to share a room. But in my day we went to summer camp where we shared a barrack room – all twenty or thirty of us. And it was our job to keep the place absolutely spick and span. The total compliment of the summer camp would be in the order of 100 to 150 cadets. This would be made up of four or five squadrons and rivalry between the squadrons was always fierce. There was never much time for sleep during that special week. By day we competed against each other in drill or even barrack room cleanliness – always referred to as 'bullshit' by the cadets. There were shooting and orienteering or map-reading competitions that kept each boy totally occupied every day.

At night the competitions between the squadrons was stepped up. There were the raids – under darkness – to destroy a barrack block at 2 or 3 o'clock in the morning with the full knowledge that a formal inspection of that block would almost certainly be made at 7.30 or 8 o'clock that day. We would foray into another squadron's block and set about destroying the neat and tidy order that prevailed there. Then they would return the compliment by wrecking our own barracks. After such high jinks, and with only two or three hours to go before inspection, we spent the rest of the night polishing and repairing and making things look new once more. It was in those early days that I learned all the tricks of the trade – using boot polish to get rid of scratches on doors or toothpaste to fill up holes in walls.

Then there was the ever-popular initiation ceremony – known as 'blackings' among the boys. Months before going away to camp some of the boys would already be looking on with fear and trepidation to their own inevitable initiation into this hallowed society. You would vow not to go to sleep even for half an hour when arriving at camp. But sleep took over in the end until, at some hour in the night, you would be woken by four or five burly young men pinning you to your bed. If you were sensible, you did not bother to put up much of a fight, which never failed to disappoint those administering the 'treatment'.

I can remember trying my best to resist their attack upon my person, but to no avail. Despite putting up a struggle, I went the way of all newcomers to this embarrassing ritual. And as the years went on it became my turn to administer the punishment to other nervous young lads. There was nothing at all personal about this. It was just one of those things that had to be done. And when it was all over the victims simply scurried off to the communal washrooms nervously hiding their genitals smeared with shiny black boot polish heralding that a good night's work had been done. There was always a feast of emotions involved. First the embarrassment and hurt that you had been invaded in such a personal way and at such a tender stage of your puberty. But above all it meant that you were now a full member of that highly prestigious club and it felt great. There you were in the washroom standing shoulder to shoulder with the next man, staring him in the face as best you could while discreetly trying to restore your private parts to the colour that nature intended.

Without ever wanting to appear the least bit racist, I can recall a couple of years later how a young Jamaican lad was initiated in the same way using training shoe whitener – no one escaped. We read in the press now about these initiation ceremonies in cadet organisations and in the army youth teams with all kinds of outrage usually ending in a court martial. But these rituals have gone on for years and years. I would suggest that rituals of some sort have gone on within the armed forces since the beginning of time and I just can't accept that there is any lasting detriment to any other than the weak few. I am delighted that my son is an air cadet and I dare say that he will go through a similar initiation to the one I did. Some things in life change at the speed of light while others in fact change very little.

I remember summer camp at RAF Leuchars in the summer of 1965. It was a glorious time. I was just approaching my fifteenth birthday and my pals, Bob and Graham, were on the camp as well. There was also someone called Gorin who was several feet taller and weighed twice as much as the rest of us – he was a hefty lad.

That start of summer camp will never leave my memory. It was an adventure right from the very beginning. We had to be at Birmingham New Street Station at 1.10 a.m., with other cadets from different stations, standing on the platform in our various squadrons, formed up by non-commissioned officers. The officers themselves were ferreting around trying to appear unconcerned but obviously very aware of the near-uncontrolled excitement in the ranks of boys. I remember getting into our allocated carriage – one of those glorious old train coaches where six passengers sat together in the confines of a private apartment. Of course, as mere air cadets we were expected to cram into that space some eight or ten deep. But it didn't matter, it was all part of the adventure. We had read and heard others talk about troop trains and now here we were on a troop train allocated to the Warwickshire and Birmingham Wing Air Cadets heading off to Royal Air Force Leuchars in Fife, Scotland.

We had been on the train no more than five minutes when Gorin – this man mountain – appeared clutching two smallish mirrors.

'Where did you get those from?' asked Bob. It transpired he had relieved them from the ladies' loo for no reason other than vandalising the train gave him something to do. We managed to persuade him that they really ought to be replaced and we helped him secure the things back in their rightful position. When we got off the train in Scotland it was left reasonably intact despite the number of pillow fights after the officers adjourned to the buffet car to allow us to let off a bit of steam.

It was several hours after leaving the West Midlands that we eventually pulled into St Andrew's Halt that was in fact RAF Leuchars. The station itself was equipped with English Electric Lightning. Seventy-four Squadron was based there and each aircraft had its own tiger's head painted on the tail. They were known as the Tiger Squadron.

I'd been an air cadet for almost a year so I'd gained a lot more practical knowledge about the Air Force and its make up. Now here I was, a young lad no more than fifteen years of age and I was standing within a few feet of fighter pilots and fighter aircraft as I strolled around

14

in my uniform on one of the front line NATO stations. I couldn't understand why every single one of my school mates did not have a burning desire to be there with me. I felt so utterly privileged that I was at a loss as to why all the lads I knew at home did not share my passion.

One evening during that camp, Graham and I went for a walk along the airfield. Those were the days when RAF fighters used to be parked in a long line on the concrete, before the idea that it might be better to hide them away in hardened aircraft shelters and disperse them all over the airfield. These were parked in a beautiful line accurate to a millimeter. As Graham and I wandered along this line we had an overwhelming urge to tough each aircraft as we walked along.

We were oblivious to the fact that we had probably broken through at least a couple of security cordons. But we were brought back down to earth minutes later when a Land Rover raced along the tarmac, screeched to a halt beside us and three military policemen climbed out. They approached us in a cautious fashion from what seemed like all sides; I suppose they were assessing whether or not we were armed and dangerous. Of course we were merely frightened young men who had suddenly realised we were well out of our depth and would have been delighted to have been driven back to our temporary barracks and left to forget the entire incident.

I am sure the military policemen capitalised on our fear but we were eventually bundled into their Land Rover to be driven across to the air crew room. It was funny how twenty years later I would find myself in a similar crew room talking to other young air cadets eager for their first taste of flying. But here we were at the wrong end of the Air Force hoping and praying that we would not be simply chucked out for our apparent misdemeanour.

We were frog marched into the crew room and I can remember an officer standing ahead of us with his hands placed on his hips. He said: 'My name is Pilot Officer Morgan and can you tell me what the hell you are doing here?'

Graham and I took turns to trip over each other's tongues in our fumbling attempts to apologise and beg forgiveness. We were sorry for what we had done and assured the pilot officer that we had meant no harm to the aircraft and that all we wanted to do was to touch them. Morgan found this highly amusing but nonetheless he was stern with us and ordered us to wash up all the coffee and tea mugs in the crew room. We did this with joy and delight, especially when we discovered that each mug was printed with the name of an individual Lightning crew member. He probably did not understand what this meant to us lads but we would have happily stood there washing up for the next ten years; the thought that Lightning fighter pilots drank out of those very mugs sent us into seventh heaven.

As soon as Morgan decided we had learned our lesson we were marched out onto the pan where he sat us both into a Lightning aeroplane and talked us through the flight deck and the instruments and controls. He explained every detail of the aircraft's performance. I cannot remember a single word that he said but I do remember just sitting there in a fighter and thinking that there was no place on earth that I would rather be.

I remember that the accommodation blocks at Leuchars were extremely spartan. They were barrack blocks that had been divided by brickwork to house five or six chaps in each section. The divisions rose to a height of about six or seven feet and then there was a gap to the ceiling. Inevitably as you lay in your narrow bed reading a magazine or writing a letter home a bucket of filthy water would come splashing over the wall soaking you where you lay below. It was down to that individual to clean and dry the blankets and sheets. Of course the only satisfaction gained from this was to tip a similar bucket of slop back over the wall onto whoever was lying there.

By day we were engaged in fierce competition of an official nature and by night the competition continued in an unofficial manner. I feel that during those early years as an air cadet we advanced by two or three years beyond our real ages. In my days as a fourteen-year-old I was as mature in many ways as a sixteen- or seventeen-year-old lad – only my lack of success in chasing the girls betrayed my age.

All of those non-commissioned lads who were only a year or two older than us were already down at the pub sinking a few beers and they would come back to camp absolutely plastered. Uniform made us look older but our metabolism remained the same so in some cases a couple of glasses of cider would leave many of those fifteen-year-olds nursing very sore heads the next morning. As we all tucked into our greasy bacon and two-egg rations served to us in the airmen's mess we had no sympathy for them. But it wouldn't be too long before I would discover for myself exactly how the older lads felt after a night on the town.

I can recall sitting up for hours bulling my boots. We bought our drill boots from the Millets store in Birmingham. They were government surplus store boots with hob-nails, thick soles and horse-shoe heels so that if you dug your heels in really hard the sparks would fly. There were a regulation number of eyelets – I think seven – and when brand new they had a rippled effect so we use to burn them to get them to shine like a mirror. Burning boots was a very delicate art; first they would be smothered in black Kiwi polish then, with a silver spoon handle heated to almost red-hot, you pushed hard against the toe cap before carefully working around the whole of the boot. Those young cadets who wanted to shine out above the rest would spend hours with a tin of polish and a hot spoon, vanishing in a cloud of black and rather pleasant smelling wax. After the waxing it was necessary to rub more polish in tiny circles using cotton wool or a yellow duster until eventually the shine would start to come through.

Among the high jinks that we indulged in, like destroying another cadet's bedpack, luggage or wardrobe, there was one golden rule that we all honoured – never touch another cadet's boots. We learned all the tricks of the trade that our own fathers and grandfathers had regaled us with from their own National Service days and we became past masters at trying to keep our own uniform slightly smarter than the next man's. These tricks included putting soap on the inside creases of trousers so that when you ironed your trousers with a damp face cloth it would moisten the soap and stick the creases together in a sharp line. The next move up was to use a razor to shave away some of the fabric on the inside of the crease in the trousers to give them just that bit more of an edge.

But some of our efforts became embarrassing failures. There was a craze for a while of using floor polish to produce an even brighter shine on our drill boots. The trouble started if it rained and our boots would disappear in a cloud of foaming lather. And if the sun was a bit too bright one day, our boots turned a delightful blue.

There really was no way of getting off too lightly. The old methods were always the best, as one young lad discovered when he tried very hard to get the best creases in his uniform trousers. Instead of using soap inside the creases he experimented with some household adhesive. Of course he had to push very hard to get his legs into the trousers at all. The glue had spread and almost sealed up the trouser legs. To the amusement of us all, as he marched out on parade the next morning he looked absolutely ridiculous.

I can remember a night exercise during our summer camp at RAF Leuchars. When I look back on it now it was probably a very dangerous event. We were divided into groups of eight or ten cadets and we had to get from one point to another through a minefield of officers and civilian instructors trying to find us.

There were all sorts of pitfalls designed to trap us. We had to wade up to our chests and armpits in mud and marshland, sneak along the beach while the tide was coming in with very little to help us along our way apart from the moonlight. Naturally if we had shone a torchlight we would have been pounced upon by those searching for us. It was very exciting for us.

There is no way that cadets today would be expected to go through this kind of exercise, it would not be allowed because somebody somewhere would be held to account if one cadet suffered so much as a scratched finger. I dare say one or two of us did suffer injury or accidents; inevitably on a summer camp there were a handful of casualties like a broken arm, a couple of broken legs and the odd illnesses. I recall one or two of the older lads engaged in a liaison with a local filly of a certain reputation and they probably went home with a few penicillin shots in their backsides and something to explain to their mothers. But

19

that is what happened in the sixties and for me they were glorious years.

I remember on the summer camp that there was a prize for the best cadet which was always a trip in a Lightning. I worked, Graham and Bob worked and as far as I can recall most of the cadets worked like stink to win that prize. I won't say all of them did because some of the air cadets had no desire to fly aeroplanes; I could never understand them at all.

It was a big disappointment when I wasn't picked that year. There was no reason why I should have been as I'd only been in the cadets a year. But I think the chap who eventually won the trip deserved it. He was called Paul and when he came back we all listened to every word he had to say. He had to fly that trip again and again as we hung on to his every word; how he had felt sick and how his stomach had been on the floor and then left in the sky as he came back down to earth. He had been punched and pushed about but had loved every second of the flight. I knew how he felt, even though I had not yet experienced it. And his encounter made me determined to fly in a Lightning.

One of my earliest heroes was a chap called Paul Page. He was a cadet corporal in my squadron and he always wore his beret at a slightly different angle to the rest. If the truth were known he was probably a good deal scruffier than the rest of the guys, but he had a certain impish magnetism that drew so many people to him and he certainly had an obvious natural quality of leadership. But one of the things about him that I admired the most was the wings badge he wore that signalled he had gained the enviable flying scholarship. He wore a brevet very similar to an RAF pilot's wings badge and in the middle it had the initials 'FS' standing for flying scholarship.

The competition to earn this scholarship was very keenly fought. Each year only twenty or so cadets would be awarded the flying hours to secure a private pilot's licence. Naturally it was assumed that those few cadets would then go on to join the forces as a pilot. However, Paul Page already had this badge; it was the first one I'd ever seen and I envied him for it. Several years later I was to wear one myself with equal pride.

Paul was also an amusing character. He tried to get into the Royal Air Force shortly after being awarded his flying scholarship but he was turned down; I'm not sure why. So he left England and went to live in Australia – I think he went to work for Ford of Australia. The last I heard about him was that he had become a wing commander in the Royal Australian Air Force where he was flying helicopters. I wish him every success.

Without getting too philosophical, one of the things that I still find difficult to rationalise was the attitude I had towards the air cadets and my membership of it compared to the attitude I had outside of the air cadets. As an air cadet I was a disciplined youngster and I took great pride in my personal appearance. I recognised my position and accepted without question that the officers were always called 'Sir' and were to be obeyed. It followed that the decisions they made or orders they gave were to be acted upon by me. Equally as I advanced through the air cadet movement and took responsibility myself I assumed the same role of unquestioned authority.

Outside of the air cadets I was nothing short of a hooligan. I was always getting into scrapes at school, and around our neighbourhood I gained notoriety as an out-of-control thug, as someone who lacked discipline or respect for authority.

I can remember specific instances which perhaps had a very strong influence on the way my character was to develop. Shortly after starting at Coleshill grammar school in Warwickshire I was asked to write an essay about my thoughts and experiences on my first day at the school. I really threw myself into the piece as I wrote the words down on paper and handed it in. It was read out in class and I felt proud that the English mistress had picked out my work. It was nice to receive such an accolade and it made me keen to do well.

I put hours of effort into the subsequent homework writing about my village. I was thrilled when my work was again read out by the English mistress. But my pride evaporated as I realised Miss Evans had only picked out my work to announce to the rest of the class that it was the most worthless piece of drivel she had ever had the misfortune to read. She was probably right, but to have shown me up in front of all my school chums I thought and still think was unforgivable.

I am sure that incident marked the end of any hopes that I may have excelled at school. I never did homework for Miss Evans again. I was a scruff at school, I threw my school uniform on and wore the same shirt for days on end, nearly always leaving my tie at home. I did my best to look my worst; anything to buck the system rather than support it.

I can clearly recall another incident in the early sixties in which I was involved along with my friends Alan Whittacker and Peter Meeson. The school was having a new annexe built comprising another twelve or so classrooms, a smart new staff room and offices. The ground floor had been completed and was now occupied while the second floor remained a building site and of course was strictly out of bounds. This meant that the unfinished floor was like a magnet to the likes of me and my partners in crime. One day we found ourselves up there and were fooling around with the dumper truck which we had managed to get started. For some reason we aimed this thing at the end of the extension and as it slowly chugged along at no more than 2 miles an hour we fled in the opposite direction to establish our alibis.

Before we even reached the ground floor there was a sickening crash as the truck just fell off the end of the building. We had successfully ruined several thousands of pounds worth of equipment and not one us gave a damn about the consequences.

The handful of lads, including myself, who had been marked down as troublemakers had our own code of conduct. It was necessary to turn out for school wearing the scruffiest blazer possible. That didn't mean to say that it needed to be covered in school dinners and ink but it had to be threadbare showing the wear and tear of several school terms of hard play. One of our crowd committed the cardinal sin of allowing his mum to buy him a new blazer. I will admit that the old one was in a pretty sorry state but that didn't let him off having a new blazer.

During a chemistry lesson in the school's lab, Whittacker and I set about rectifying the situation. Armed with our wash bottles, which were generally filled with water, we discreetly moved in on our chum pouring the contents of the wash bottles into his pockets. He caught us doing this about halfway through our mission and he shared the joke, believing he was the victim of a fairly mild prank to christen his new blazer. What he hadn't realised was that his pockets contained sulphuric acid and it was with great joy and mirth that Whittacker and I spent the rest of the lesson watching the hated new blazer dissolve before our very eyes. He returned home that evening with his new – and expensive – school blazer in tatters and was at his desk the next morning wearing the old one.

For as long as I can remember I've been fascinated by the power of explosives and along with a couple of friends, Graham Andrew and Peter Yates, began feverishly to read up on the subject. We used to carry out our own practical experiments starting off in a very small way and graduating to some really quite dramatic efforts that went bump in the night and in the day.

We made our explosives from household constituents with a mixture of weedkiller and sugar that would produce the explosive effect almost of gunpowder. This, confined in some sort of makeshift shell or other and then heated from the outside with a paraffin-soaked rag would produce the most dramatic results. I used to get the piping for the shells from my dad's workshop. Dad being a builder, it was dead easy for me to get hold of lengths of copper tubing without him knowing too much about it. First we would saw the copper tubing into lengths of about three or four inches, hammer one end over, fill the tube with our compound and hammer the other end over to seal it. Then we would apply heat to the outside of the tube and stand back to watch a small clod of turf or some other object go bang.

The early and small explosions inevitably led to more ambitious projects. I suppose the intermediate stage was when we would get a length of tubing, now about a foot long, and strap it to a tree. Once again the soaked paraffin rag was put on the outside of the tube before lighting the rag, retiring and watching as the tree collapsed with shock. We regarded ourselves as the amateur lumberjacks of a suburb of Birmingham.

It didn't stop there and as we became more accomplished we moved on to bigger objects until eventually we almost met our demise. I had secured some really rather thick tubing from Dad's supplies. It was much bigger than we had used in our previous experiments. We decided we were going to make 'Big Bertha' and see if we could blow a large tree down.

The garden shed round at Peter's house was now the operations room for the junior explosives team. We hammered over one end of the tube, filled it with the compound and started to hammer the other end over as the tube was held in a vice. After a few minutes of hammering Peter, who was holding one end of the tube, noticed that our homemade bomb was getting rather hot. Graham and I felt it and agreed things were getting uncomfortably warm. We all took one look at each other before the three of us were out of the shed door and running for all we were worth. The next second there was the most horrendous bang and the majority of what was left of the garden shed went right over the top of Pete Yates' house and ended up in his front garden. Peter has gone on to become a respected and respectable optician and Graham became a government scientist, having spent some years in nuclear research. Those early experimental days must have come in handy for Graham.

For a while in my teens I used to work evenings and weekends at a filling station as a forecourt attendant in the days before before it all became self-service. There were a number of fringe benefits to working in the filling station, not least because I got 'free' petrol for my motorcycle. The other was that we seemed to be able to get hold of old cars at a rate just about as fast as we could wreck them. Now I look back on some of the cars that we smashed to smithereens, I realise that they would be quite valuable today.

I remember once again the trio of Graham, Peter and myself in a Sunbeam Talbot that one of our forecourt customers had given us having bought himself a brand new Triumph Herald. We took it over to a local field and duly drove around having a great time. After a while just driving around the field got a little boring so we spiced things up with a few stunts – driving the car into trees and jumping out at the last minute. Sometimes we had more than one car, driving them at each other and then jumping out at the last minute. Needless to say after a while the last minute didn't exist and so there would be two cars being driven hell for leather at each other over the rough field. The inevitable crash of bumpers caused a few chest pains and some bruising but usually very little else. There was always the odd broken limb or a sprained wrist or something but no one ever got horribly injured or at least no one in my team. It was not uncommon to read in the papers about some lad with his own private home explosive kit blowing a hand or a foot off. Quite obviously if that had happened to me then my whole life would have changed because I needed all my faculties, both physical and mental to pursue my chosen career.

Of the other little fringe benefits on our petrol forecourt, now that I think back on it, I would admit to one or two of them being on the shady side. There was a man who came to see us, usually about every two or three weeks, and from him we would buy wrist watches at amazingly attractive prices. We would have no trouble in offloading our chosen selection around the Birmingham pubs on a Friday and

Saturday night. In fact we started wholesaling as people realised the bargains they were getting and bought from us in bulk. We built up a regular clientele; they sold the watches on and we collected a handsome profit from our own mark up.

The boss at our garage got a little bit annoyed with us at one stage when, as a side line, we started selling cut flowers as well as the petrol. That was until he realised that the cut flowers were easily bringing in people to buy petrol so we were allowed to continue the trade.

I say 'we' because Graham was the petrol forecourt manager for quite a while in between studying for his O' and A' levels at school. He used to rush back on his motorcycle at lunch time to cash up and change shifts. The filling station was certainly one of the larger ones on the east side of Birmingham, and it was run by a young man who was just sixteen years old.

The more I look back on my early life the more certain I become that I would have gone into a life of crime had I not been accepted as a pilot in the RAF. As a youngster I had a driven need to be excited and to enjoy excitement. It was fairly easy to come by in a number of ways, some of them not terribly legal or safe. As a teenager during the early sixties there were two main youth cultures: the Mods and the Rockers, and I was most definitely a Rocker. Those ridiculous scooters ridden by the Mods were for woolly woofters and for wrecking with large spanners!

As I approached my sixteenth birthday it was with a fairly tentative approach that I tackled my mum and dad about the prospect of my owning a motorbike. Strangely enough it was Mum who said 'Yes' almost straight away but Dad had tremendous reservations. He would not be moved and it was not until I brought out the family photograph albums and showed him the proud pictures of him collecting numerous trophies and prize monies from his speedway racing days that he had to agree that his argument was based entirely on 'Do as I say and not do as I do'.

The first motorbike I ever rode was as a result of a little connivance. My friend Graham also wanted to buy a motorcycle and as he was the same vintage as me we checked the small adverts in the papers together before setting off to view one in nearby Tamworth. Graham actually wanted to buy the bike and I had told him I could already ride one. In fact I had never been on a motorbike in my life. We stood around this machine and I made what I thought were knowledgeable grimaces.

There was little about the bike that made much sense to me apart from its colour. But Graham seemed impressed by it and so did the man who was selling the bike. I can recall being surprised that he wanted to sell it as he seemed to like the bike so much. However, £25 changed hands. I got astride and kickstarted it only to kangaroo off into the middle distance. Luckily I was entirely alone but during that ten-mile or so journey from Tamworth to Castle Bromwich I learnt to ride a motorbike at someone else's expense, fortunately without disastrous results.

Graham and I shared his bike; he was extemely generous that way and whenever he wasn't riding it and for the price of a gallon of petrol, he loaned it to me. Having finally convinced my father that I should have a motorbike of my own, it was my turn to scour the area for my dream machine. The first bike I ever bought I first spotted in a car showroom in Aston. It was in fact a bigger and more powerful machine than I was legally allowed to ride before I had passed my test so I borrowed Graham's bike to take and pass my test, then become the proud owner of a BSA B40.

I quickly graduated, through various swaps and some roadside dealing, to a BSA Road Rocket which I rode with great skill and fairly regularly came off as I roared around the villages of south Warwickshire. I particularly remember one accident I had and thinking back it was probably the first time that I ever came really close to meeting my maker. Of course, by virtue of my lifestyle I have since been uncomfortably close on several other occasions. This time I was riding back home from my girlfriend's house. There was a long uphill straight culminating at the top with a kink in the road that was quite difficult to negotiate at high speeds. Needless to say it was one of those bends that most of the motorcycling fraternity had claimed to have achieved a certain speed taking.

So it was in the evening on my way home and time to try to beat the speed. By my own standards I was going fairly fast, probably just nudging 80mph. I came upon the bend and roared around it before straightening up the bike but there to my horror, right in front of me with no place to go, was a double-decker bus. It was one of those old-fashioned buses like the London red bus where the rear quarter section has a platform with a hand rail and a spiral staircase to the first floor. The conductor normally stood on the platform.

I slammed my brakes full on as my bike began to perform like a bucking bronco. The bus ahead of me was so close it seemed like the biggest building I had ever seen. There was a furious squealing of tyres and a gnashing of gears and the bike eventually stopped just inches from the bus platform. I deftly stepped from the bike on to the stationary bus and asked the astonished conductor the price of a single fare to

Birmingham. My bike was still in one piece and, thankfully, so was I.

I really do envy the young motorcyclists of today with their hi-tech machines. The bikers themselves are clad in regulation safety helmets, padded leather jackets and trousers. I mostly roared around in a pair of sawn-off Levi's and a long-sleeved T-shirt. I enjoyed the immunity of youth but I had my spills like the rest. I've wound up in a field or picked myself up in someone's front garden, usually with no more than a few scratches.

My girlfriend's father sensibly refused to allow me to take her for a spin. When he finally relented, having convinced him of my road worthiness, I bought her a new crash helmet. We mounted up for our first outing on the bike together and about four miles down the road I hit a burst water main and came off. She survived without a scratch apart from two gaping holes in a brand new pair of jeans as I lay in the road with a chunk of chrome handlebar sticking into my knee.

Shortly after my seventeenth birthday it was time to take my driving test. It never occurred to me that I would fail. I had been driving cars since I was eleven years old and it used to be a favourite Sunday treat. My dad would have his game of darts and a couple of pints of beer in the pub and we would sit in the garden with a glass of Vimto and a packet of crisps. When it was time to go home we would make our usual detour to the local disused airfield at Castle Bromwich. Dad would move over into the passenger seat and I would be allowed to drive his car around the airfield.

I inquired at the local motoring school about the number of official lessons I must have before being legally allowed to take the test. It was three and I paid £5.0s.3d for three lessons in three different cars. Then off I went to take and pass my driving test.

Dad and I decided to set up a little business together maintaining factory and warehouse roofs in the area. We soon started to attract the work making good money. Inevitably the access to cash went to my head and I became blasé about meeting deadlines and even turning up for work. I lost a good few contracts and let a lot of people down, not least myself.

Then there was the café bistro project that I started up with my girlfriend's cousin. He managed to raise the cash – he was a couple of years older than me and already had a job as a cinema manager. I had some ideas and we roped in another pal, Lawrence, to get the business off the ground. We set up our bistro close to home and waited for the profits to start rolling in. The whole thing was a failure from start to finish. We had installed this tremendous light show which unfortunately chucked out enough heat to turn the place into a sauna. So we had to install air conditioning. By the end of the day the electricity bill alone meant that, to break even, we had to sell a cup of coffee for every minute that we were open. It was impossible and the bistro was opened and closed down in less than six months.

I then worked for a time at a firm called Minworth Metals and Alloys, working with a high-temperature gas torch to cut lumps of metal down into smaller chunks ready for melting down and reprocessing. The conditions were appalling but the money was fantastic. There were five of us working in a filthy, muddy yard full of scrap steel and we were paid for the amount of steel we had cut.

There was a canal that ran alongside the factory separated by a six-foot high fence. Myself and a workmate called Adrian would corner any large chunks of phosphor bronze or copper and any other valuable non-ferrous metals we had spotted. When no one was watching we would fling them over the fence onto the canal tow path. I had already acquired a small canal boat moored just a few miles along the waterway. By the time we had loaded up our spoils there would be very little distance between the water line and the gunnels of the boat as we went off with our contraband. At that time phosphor bronze made about £50 a hundredweight and more than doubled my wages at Minworth Metals and Alloys.

There were other incidents that occurred at Minworth Metals and Alloys, mostly as a result of my pursuit of science. I can remember an old treacle experiment that we used to do at school which caused an explosion created by an evacuated atmosphere. Without becoming too technical, this was done using coal gas and a treacle tin which eventually went pop. At the scrapyard one day I tried it out with a bottle of acetylene gas, a bottle of oxygen gas and a very long piece of plastic tubing that was about six foot in length. It caused the most horrendous explosion, and there was scrap metal spread as far as the eye could see. There were also a lot of very anxious faces in that yard, including one sacked Pablo Mason who went on to become a hamper packer. The money was appalling but the conditions were a damn sight more comfortable.

A regular weekend activity as an air cadet was air experience gliding. My own squadron's gliding school, which was shared with the other Warwickshire squadrons, was 633 Squadron Gliding School at Cosford just out-side Wolverhampton. The 633 Squadron had been made famous by the fictional RAF flyers already written about and filmed. We air cadets took great pleasure in assuming the title and being part of the same legendary squadron.

The unit had its core of officers, the CO being a character called George Crump. He was a very upper-crust sort of chap and certainly looked the part. I don't know what he did in civilian life but wearing an RAF blue uniform he looked every bit like a Second World War fighter pilot. He was an extremely capable aviator. The system of launching the gliders at Cosford was by a winch that is basically a drum connected through a gearbox to a diesel engine. The whole thing looks like a big tractor. Around the drum is wound a mile or so of wire cable which is attached to the glider. As the glider is pulled along and becomes airborne, the pilot pulls a handle releasing the cable as soon as he feels he has gained enough height and is being pulled earthwards again instead of into the sky. The cable then falls back to the ground and is towed back by Land Rover to launch another waiting aircraft.

The officers at the school were also volunteers and most of them were civilians who dedicated their spare time to us. The real work at cadet school was carried out by staff cadets who had shown an aptitude after they had completed a gliding course. After a couple of years as an air cadet I joined their ranks and went on to assist in the day-to-day running of the school. For me it was an adventure playground. We were all little more than sixteen years old and, along with flying the gliders with younger cadets, we were allowed to drive four-ton lorries around the base as we ferried the younger ones to and from a lunch break.

I completed my gliding course in 1967, just before my sixteenth birthday. The flying didn't thrill me as it had some of the other boys who would have killed to get another trip. I was dying to move on to jet-propelled aircraft as I found gliding restrictive and slightly pedestrian. I certainly enjoyed the flights and did not find the technique too difficult. I did about twenty flights with an instructor at hand to practise launching and handling the machine on a flying circuit of about one thousand feet. One of the more exacting operations was to land the aircraft properly. Of course, when you are coming into land you cannot just put the power on and come round again for a second try. In a glider it has to be right every time, you don't get a second chance. As we became more accomplished we would show off our skills. I have seen a Coke tin knocked off the top of a concrete tier by the wing tip of a glider. The pilot involved let go of the winch at about one thousand feet and then dived towards the ground to flick the tin away before he pulled back up into the sky. We were hugely impressed but in fact that boy was nothing short of stupid and could have so easily got it wrong.

I can recall so many instances where guys just push it that little too far. They are never around to explain what went wrong during the last few minutes. I first realised that flying is not all blue sky and bliss during a gliding week at Halesland Ridge, a site near to RAF Locking in Avon. The course was held every year and the more accomplished aviators went along. After some training in a twin seater you went off to fly solo.

The ridge site relied heavily on an updraught from the prevailing wind that actually hit the hill. This air would carry on upwards to the gliding site itself which was based at the top of the hill. We launched using the traditional winch and once airborne we could fly out over the low ground still relying on a constant updraught of air to keep the glider in the sky. One of the more advanced qualifications for our gliding certificates was to remain airborne for a protracted length of time. We were all quite happy to show off our log books detailing that we had managed to stay up in the sky for several hours at a time.

One particular day there was very little lift from the hill and we had to work very hard to stay airborne more than a few minutes before being forced to come back to the ridge and land. I watched in horror as one of the gliders gradually got lower and lower over the ridge site. Instead of sticking to the rules of guidance to fly away from the ridge and land in the nearest field, he kept on going. As we stood by the tea wagon we could see he was determined to try to land at the ridge. He must have panicked because the glider suddenly flicked right over going into a sickening downwards spiral to the ground. There was the sound of a horrible crunch just a mile or so away from us as his glider seemed to dismantle itself.

I and a few others scrambled aboard a Land Rover to make our way to where he had crashed. There was that terrible fear of wanting to help but the horror of stumbling upon the awful remains of one of our fellow cadets. You don't want to run ahead for fear of what you may encounter in the cockpit. In fact I was one of the first ones to be physically sick. I can remember arriving at the scene to encounter a rather dazed individual sitting in what was left of his cockpit. He was swearing like mad but it was all a muddle because he was half asleep, clearly in a state of shock. When he was taken by ambulance to the nearest hospital he was found to have a fractured collar bone and a massively dented ego. As far as I know that cadet never flew an aircraft again. In the years ahead I would find myself much closer to aviation carnage. During one week of my advanced flying training I attended five funerals.

During my youth I also developed a passion for aircraft

spotting. My pal Graham knew everything there was to know about the aircraft that flew our skies. As a boy, he dreamed of becoming a pilot but his eyesight was hopeless and he stood no chance. When we were twelve, he and I travelled the country adding aircraft registrations to our 'Ian Allen' log books. We used the old trick; he told his parents he was staying at our house while mine thought I was spending the night at Graham's. We'd meet up at 2 o'clock in the morning outside the Bradford Arms pub and then hitch a ride with an all-night lorry driver. Within a few hours we'd be standing on the rooftop viewing balcony of the Queen's building at Heathrow noting down the registrations of every aircraft that taxied down the runway.

Graham and I came close to seeing every one of the British European Airways aircraft. I think I had only two missing from my log book and I can recall that one of them was 'golf-alpha-papa-echo-echo'. This aircraft was a Vanguard and it eventually crashed at Heathrow on Boxing Day in the early sixties with the loss of a number of lives. After that incident I lost my appetite for plane-spotting and Graham and I called it a day.

With the air cadets I was fortunate to spend weekends at RAF Shawbury near Shrewsbury in Shropshire. We would sit in the back of a De Havilland Chipmunk and spend the next half an hour or so being thrown around in the sky. Now this was getting so much closer to where I really wanted to be. Within seconds of my first flight in a Chipmunk I was totally committed to becoming an RAF pilot. Everything about the aircraft seemed right to me; the smell, the sensation and the feeling of supremacy. It wasn't just that this is where I wanted to be but where I had to be.

One of the courses available to just a handful of the cadets each year was the flying scholarship. For this you were required to attend the officer and air crew selection centre at RAF Biggin Hill having been recommended by your squadron commander. After a series of exacting selection procedures you would spend thirty hours' flying training at one of the RAF's flying schools. There were hundreds of eager hopefuls pleading for a place on this course and I was over the moon when I discovered I had been selected for 'Airwork Services' training in Perth, Scotland, where I would hopefully complete a flying scholarship.

On one desperately cold and early morning in March 1970, at nineteen years of age, I found myself on a windswept platform at Perth railway station. There were two other people already on the platform and another elderly station worker laboriously sweeping around the Edwardian lamp posts. Standing there in my smart cadet's uniform I asked him for the directions to Scone. He stopped his sweeping and with a look of disgust he replied: 'It's Skoon, Laddie, fucking Skoon!' He certainly put me in my place.

The school at Perth was renowned as an excellent flying training school and its role was divided between the RAF, a large contingent of overseas pupils and British Airways students. The foreign influence at the school meant there was always a rather exotic flavour to canteen menus. Amazingly, Perth was where I developed an enduring taste for curry. I had never tasted a proper meat Madras before but from the first mouthful I was addicted.

After two weeks of class work I was finally allowed to try my skills in the air. On 2 April 1970 my instructor sent me up on my very first solo flight. It was just one circuit around the airfield in a powered aircraft – a Cessna 150 – but it was sheer joy to me. At the end of the month I had completed the required thirty-five hours of flying to gain my private pilot's licence. I still have that piece of paper showing my licence number 90765. I am still very proud of that early achievement. Now I was on my way to officer selection in the RAF.

Both officer and air crew selection took place at RAF Biggin Hill in Kent, the home of so many brave Battle of Britain pilots. Those selection procedures had changed so little from the days when flyers were being recruited as Second World War fighter pilots. In fact many of the reaction and co-ordination tests had survived from the late thirties.

At the 'OASC', as the selection centre was known, I considered my chances to be an odds-on certainty. I had already sailed through my air cadet training, I'd earned a flying scholarship and had passed through all the selection procedures that I believed would guarantee me a place as a pilot in the RAF. Until then I had achieved everything that I had wanted to. I had passed my driving test first time and I'd even gained a modest five O' levels at school, despite my reluctance to do any work.

But after two and a half days at Biggin Hill I was to receive the biggest setback to my ambitions. In fact I had to wait four nail-biting weeks before I heard back from the RAF. As I read the letter of rejection I was, for the first time, overwhelmed by a sense of devastation. It did not just read that my services would not be required for the time being, it informed me that I need not even bother to reapply.

After a few days of misery I wrote back to the selectors at Biggin Hill declaring that I refused to take no for an answer. To my surprise and enormous relief, I received a reply telling me that I should find other work for the next two years and then reapply. The letter made it clear that should I then be lucky it would be because I could prove to the recruiting officers that I had grown up. For the first time in my life I reflected on my own actions and behaviour, and for the next two years I threw myself into hard work. I studied engineering at college during the evenings and kept down a good job in factory management during the day.

Two years on I nervously arrived at Biggin Hill. I knew this would be my last chance to prove my worth. In the leadership tests I listened, watched others and considered my own views before rushing in and showing myself up. I had matured during the two years I had waited in hope that the RAF would want me. When I arrived for that second attempt I made sure that I made the right comments at the right time and appeared in front of the examiners to be hardworking and serious about my intentions, and confident about who and what I was.

Well, it worked and a couple of weeks after leaving Biggin Hill I received a letter inviting me to join the service. And in fact I delayed my own date of joining by about eight months because I wanted to complete my evening course at college which I was already halfway through.

But despite my new-found maturity, I don't think that earlier experience of near-failure did anything to dampen my sense of fun. On my second attempt I had once again passed through the medical phase of the tests when I bumped into a chap who was about to be called in for the eye test. I had just completed the examination and passed all the tests. This poor guy knew that he didn't have a hope – he had already chatted to me in the bar the night before and told me he needed reading glasses.

Without them he would have certainly failed. I don't even know why I risked my own chances by being found out, but I agreed to go back in there for him and take the test again in his name. If I had been caught it would have ended my hopes of a flying career in the RAF. But the ophthalmic surgeon must have had his mind on other things because Keith passed his eye test with flying colours and remarkably similar results to my own. He is still a senior officer in the RAF commanding his own fighter squadron.

2

Officer Training

I had spent nine of my teenage years as an air cadet and towards the end of that time I actually mastered the correct spelling of the title 'officer'. And just before my twenty-third birthday I finally joined those serried ranks as I began my officer training.

It was a world I never dreamed even existed. I truly felt that it must have been like joining the champagne set in high society. And I sampled life in the officers' mess with gusto with the rest of the 'boys'. We simply never went to bed until we had fallen over in the bar, too drunk to stand. Looking back I know for sure that my days as a lowly flying officer were some of the best of my life. And I know too that when I finally accepted senior promotion it was to be the greatest career mistake I ever made. I was far happier and more ably equipped to thrive as a commissioned hooligan. It was what I was good at and a job at which I was happiest.

I remember my first day in the Royal Air Force as though it were yesterday. I arrived at RAF Henlow, near Hitchin in Hertfordshire on the afternoon of 2 September 1973. I was Officer Cadet P.J.D. Mason. Within days firmly etched on my mind was my service number: 8026447. In those first days of square bashing and running up and down and getting up at all hours and filling in forms, there wasn't half an hour between someone asking for or the need to write down my number: 8026447.

As a young man I always enjoyed nice cars and motoring has been a passion of mine from an early age. On joining the Air Force I arrived at the car park at Henlow in my gleaming red TR-5A. It was about three or four years old but it absolutely shone and it was my pride and joy – I think I cared more for it than the owner who had taken delivery of it at brand new. On my arrival I parked the car in the quadrangle as I had been instructed by the NCO at the main gate. I could open the door but it was opened for me by a very smart young man who introduced himself to me as Alan Thompson. He helped carry my bags up to my designated quarter in the mess. During those first days of training we were all accommodated in dormitory-style rooms where we were required to make bedpacks and undergo spot inspections – just like my teenage years as a cadet.

Alan seemed incredibly experienced in the ways of the system and he showed me round. When I asked how long he had been there it transpired he had arrived only about an hour and a half before me. It became one of those relationships which is formed the moment you meet in that it seemed we had known each other for years within just five minutes of shaking hands. Alan is still a close friend of mine and was best man at my wedding.

I embarked on sixteen weeks of officer training. Alan had a university degree which meant that his uniform was slightly different to mine. He was a student officer and was paid the daily rate of pilot officer while I was an officer cadet and paid the lower daily rate of an airman. But if all went well in sixteen weeks' time, just before Christmas

1973, we would both graduate as officers in the Royal Air Force, Alan as an engineer and me as a student pilot.

It seemed the motto of RAF Henlow was to work hard and play hard. For me it was absolute paradise. I worked incredibly hard and I also enjoyed playing just as hard. There was quite a cross-section of society among my fellow students. I'd expected to meet a lot of upper-class people and sure enough there were many of them. But my pal, Alan, was a typical Geordie and there were lots of guys from lots of different backgrounds.

It was very amusing to see about half a dozen or so who had hair down to their shoulders and hadn't really hoisted aboard the fact that a short back and sides was certainly going to be the order of the day. Graham Morgan, who went on to fly Nimrods, arrived with hair brushing his shoulders and a guitar. He was in for quite a rude awakening over the next few days.

The daily routine was quite rigorous and was imposed upon us by the staff, and the evening routine was equally demanding although it was imposed by ourselves. Things started at about 7 o'clock in the morning with the inevitable bed to be made with its corners all but ironed into shape. Boots polished and out for a quick morning run then breakfast and onto the parade ground at 9 o'clock. We had drill every day and most of the time twice a day, marching up and down and side to side both in preparation for final graduation day which was a very grand affair and also the build up to the requirements of military discipline.

Our instructor was a flight sergeant by the name of Benjamin Britten. What an absolute character he was. While each of us was being instructed and before we were commissioned we would address him as 'Sir'. And he would address each of us in turn as either 'Sir' or

'Ma'am'. He explained the only difference would be that we would mean it.

Evening dress regulations at Henlow and in the service in which we enrolled were extremely strict by today's standards. I had bought four brand new lounge suits just before joining the service. After 7 o'clock in the evening in any of the public rooms, you had to wear a suit and tie on Mondays, Tuesdays and Thursdays. Wednesdays, Fridays and Weekend days were known affectionately as 'casual' or 'sports' days. On those occasions we wore a blazer or sports jacket and flannels, always with a tie. Whenever we were out from Henlow, even in our own time, we were required to dress smartly and we were also required to wear a Trilby which was guaranteed to make us an easy target for the local louts. Of course there was the temptation to flaunt the regulations, but certainly within a fifty-mile radius of Henlow I always conformed. It felt as though we were being watched every second of the day and even when we slept. To start with it was quite an imposition but after a very short time I just settled into the swing of the system and accepted it.

Our squadron commander of purple squadron – as my particular cadet squadron was known – meant that we were required to wear purple scarves. Of course, as a sign of loyalty we consciously wore something purple most of the time. But Squadron Commander Peter Frame was a very dapper gentleman. He was a hunter fighter pilot currently on a ground tour and just to look at him you knew he was everything that you could imagine a fighter pilot to be. And he was certainly everything that I wanted to be.

I can recall an incident when, after a few weeks' training, I had forgotten to get my hair cut and I certainly had a good deal more hair than I have now. At morning prayers, one of the first events of the day, when the squadron commander would stand in front of us to give us a broad idea of the day's events, Squadron Leader Frame commented, 'Officer Cadet Mason, get your hair cut.' Well, I forgot again and the following morning Squadron Leader Frame simply said, 'Officer Cadet Mason, I will not tell you again.'

That evening I went along to the camp barber and explained that as I had forgotten to have my hair cut the previous evening he had better do it on the short side. What I mistake I made. To a station barber a normal haircut was only about a quarter of an inch overall. To cut it short meant that it barely poked through the surface of the scalp. When I realised what he had done I didn't go to evening meal that night or to the bar, which for me was unheard of.

The following morning at prayers in the lecture room I could no longer keep my hat on. Before the staff arrived I removed my hat to the delight of my fellow cadets who roared with laughter. Squadron Leader Frame came in and ignored my shining pate completely until the very end of his morning briefing when he simply glanced across and said, 'Mason, your hair is too short. You are confined to camp for one month for dumb insolence.'

Overall the training at Henlow was excellent and looking back on it now there was obviously a need to make sure that we would conform no matter what. After all, those of us destined to become pilots may well be required to deliver nuclear weapons and given that stage of the imaginary holocaust there wouldn't be time to start asking why.

The training was hard and the physical demands on us were exacting. There were classroom lectures where we were educated on the history of the Air Force; how to write and how to communicate. There was even a week where we spent time in an office simulator where our little squadron ran its own Air Force station with its day-to-day scenarios imputed by the staff for us to deal with. There was plenty of outdoor physical exercise with poles and drums over shark-infested custard. And this time we were told how to do it. Qualities of leadership, which had been assessed during our initial selection at Biggin Hill, were now refined and honed.

The social life was really very acceptable. We were purple squadron while the others were green, yellow, red and other colours. But our squadron was particularly blessed in that it had a G Flight. Within the squadron there were flights A to G. Of course G were the girlies and our lot were particularly lovely. I'd started off on B Flight, there was no particular reason for this and no significance to the alphabetical order. But after a few weeks it was acknowledged that the ladies on G Flight lacked a little bit of muscle. They certainly had the inclination to perform the physical tasks but they simply weren't strong enough to carry them out. So Alan and I, for the final exercise of training, were transferred to become members of G Flight. At first there were cries from the other male cadets that we had become a pair of girls. But I knew exactly on which side my bread had been buttered and we had a great time. No longer did I need to spend hours at the ironing board getting my shirts and trousers ready for parade day – in exchange for a bit of spit and polish on the ladies' shoes my creases were sharper than they had ever been. I would also never deny providing a shoulder to cry on during some of those dark evenings when work had got a little bit too much and it was time for a few tears.

It was a very strict hierarchy at Henlow. The sixteen-week course meant that every four weeks a squadron would graduate. The senior squadron – the one in its last four weeks' training – really were the gods around the cadets' mess. And those in their last eight weeks of training were the demi-gods. I was quite happy to wait my turn during the early weeks and as the weeks went on and my seniority in the mess improved, I enjoyed it all the more.

The high jinks were legendary. Alan and I and one or two others popped into nearby Bedford for a couple of beers. We arrived back at the students' mess very jolly and rather late, probably well past midnight with an early morning start ahead. But the night was young and there was plenty of time to sleep. One of our group had acquired along the way a sexy pair of ladies' lace knickers. Lots were drawn and it was decided that someone had to install these knickers onto the clock on the college roof. I was that someone.

The cadets' college mess was quite a grand affair with a loft on the centre of the roof on which was the clock. The clock was always accurate but we decided it was time to stop it with the pair of knickers. With a few beers inside me the journey from the second-floor window out onto the guttering and across the tiles to reach the clock tower did not look anywhere near as daunting as it was. Alan and I finally made it onto the roof. He looked particularly silly as his hands were occupied in our ascent and the only place to hold the knickers was in his teeth. We must have been making a hell of a racket, coupled with the reassuring noises from the ground.

We eventually made it to the clock tower – some fifty feet off the ground on a frosty half-lit night. But just as we were positioning the knickers on the tower the fire bell sounded. I still don't know to this day whether it was a genuine practice or whether another member of our group had decided to liven things up. Alan and I froze, which wasn't difficult considering where we were. But only seconds after the fire bell sounded there were floodlights out on the sports field outside our mess as the rest of the cadets poured from their slumber to report for fire drill.

The ranks of squadrons were all facing the College Hall while Alan and I sat like frozen dummies on the roof. But not one of them tipped off the members of staff who were counting the ranks. In our own squadron there was a good deal of shuffling as cadets moved place to make sure an empty space where we should have been standing was not noticed. Whenever our names were called somebody would say from the back 'Here, Sir'.

During the sixteen weeks at Henlow there were two major camps; the first called eight-day camp and the second, a week or so before the end of our training, was called six-day camp. We went off to one of the numerous military training areas to carry out our exercise. There was even more shark-infested custard. On eight-day course we were taught and on six-day course we were assessed.

My eight-day camp was going very well until the end when I was made camp commandant. I made a complete and utter cock-up of my position. I got it right in the neck and was told I had better pull my socks up or I wouldn't be graduating as an officer.

When six-day camp came around I knew I would be graduating. That day came around – it was always known as Black Tuesday even though the parade itself was held on a Friday. The morning in question arrived and we all grouped in the squadron main assembly hall to be called in one by one to the flight commander's office. If you actually returned from his office to the assembly hall it was a sign you had graduated. The code that we knew was that if you went in to see the flight commander and he addressed you by your first name you knew you had graduated. If he addressed you by your rank and surname you knew you had failed and the best you could hope for was a recourse of up to three months.

My intake had 140 on day one and by graduation there were sixty or seventy of us left. My flight commander at Henlow was Flight Lieutenant Graham Erskine and his previous tour had been as a Hercules navigator. Along with Peter Frame, the squadron commander and a fighter pilot, I think they were among the few aircrew who were actually on the staff, and they stood out as a breed apart from their ground-based contemporaries.

Even during the early days of officer training those of us who were destined to become air crew were in some way different to those who would remain on the ground. Even at that early stage we were being groomed and moulded for the service that would be required from us at a later date. As the course developed and we came closer to the end, our relationship with our flight commander began to blossom. I never called him Graham until the evening of the Graduation Ball apart from one night earlier when we took part in a car treasure hunt cup rally organised by one of the other students. I asked Graham if he would be my navigator for the rally. I seem to gel with him straight away, each taking instructions and advice from the other. We were doing well until I completely misjudged a bend which he had forecast well ahead and we shot off into a field. The crops in the field slowed us down and we stopped and apart from the missing exhaust system and a few scratches to the paintwork we were completely unscathed.

Graham was a Scot with that typically dry sense of

humour. He said, 'We ought to get a move on before the rest catch us up.'

As we approached the winning line the car was making the most incredible noise. But we sat in the pub that night with a silver cup and a bottle of champagne each. The repairs to the car cost me well over a month's salary but I was simply delighted that we had won.

By graduation of Christmas 1973 we had already learned an old trick to find out if we would be making the grade. There were three tailors on the camp: Moss Bros, Allkits and RE City. It was far more than a coincidence if you went along to find your uniform was ready two weeks before graduation. If it was you were likely to be OK. If for some reason there had been a delay, it probably meant you would not be passing out. Of course the tailors offered a no-graduate no-fee deal although they hotly denied any access to inside information.

Graduation day was always an extremely moving ceremony as we marched onto the parade ground as the whole college was on parade. Those of us whose names were called out by the reviewing officer and listed as having been commissioned into the Royal Air Force marched off in slow time through the ranks of the senior support squadron who presented arms to salute us.

It was very emotional but within seconds of leaving the parade ground with our uniforms suitably adorned with white flashes to indicate a cadet, one of the first things that happened was that we removed the flashes and strutted around the base to collect as many salutes from unsuspecting airmen as we could. Suddenly we had travelled through some invisible barrier. The directing staff who had given us such a hard time through our four months of training were now to be known by their Christian names.

No more did we have to salute them. As junior officers in the Air Force it was traditional not to accept salutes from officers of a rank below flight lieutenant. We had ascended from the lowliest of the ranks to young officers deserving and commanding respect.

That night the Graduation Ball was the stuff that dreams are made of. The officers and their ladies were announced as they entered the grand hall. There was far more food than anyone of us could eat in a week let alone an evening, and the band of the Royal Air Force played for us to dance. At midnight the disco took over and we danced until dawn with a champagne breakfast on the terrace.

I glanced across to my colleagues wondering if it was all over or had it all just begun? The next day we parted with the four winds for a week or two's leave before the inevitable course beyond commissioning in the service. For me and about a third of the other guys, we would be going on to pilot training which would take us through the next two years at least. Some people would see only six weeks or so before they would be in full-time employment. Some of the airmen who were on the course would be going back to their bases as an officer, no longer an NCO.

For me the next course was the academic course at RAF Church Fenton which I started on 10 January 1974. The course was designed to sharpen us up before we went into the classroom and on to our first bouts of flying training. Within half an hour of arriving in the classroom I had taken a step back in time by thirty years. I had already completed an engineering course at technical college in Birmingham where we had dispensed with the old Imperial measures. Here was a step back in time where the tutors were as crusty as their teaching methods. But I passed the course after some of the hardest work I had done for years, even though it was written in my confidential assessments, which followed me throughout my RAF career, that I had been totally lazy and had achieved the barest minimum of standard with the barest minimum of effort. It was entirely untrue and a couple of courses later there was quite an outcry when a young man who had a mathematics and aeronautics degree actually failed the academic studies course. He simply hadn't understood the outmoded units of measurement but as he had failed the course he could not go on to flying training and was discharged from the Air Force.

After completing the academic course I was due to stay at Church Fenton and fly twenty to thirty hours on the Chipmunk, a propeller-driven light aircraft. However, after a particularly fun weekend with my girlfriend I arrived back at the base at 2 o'clock in the morning in early January 1974 to see a note pinned to my door. It read: 'Pablo, we have been trying to get hold of you all weekend and we hope it was a good one because you are due to start flying training straight on to jets at RAF Linton-on-Ouse at 8 o'clock on Monday morning.'

With no more than two or three hours to pack up my room and throw my stuff into the car I drove up the A1 to North Yorkshire to start a year's training on jets. I had only flown for about four hours total in the last couple of years and most of that in a Cessna 150. Here I was about to start my RAF flying training straight into jets. In fact it was going to be many years before I ever flew a propeller-driven aircraft again.

3

Flying Training

The base at Linton-on-Ouse was a hub of Air Force life. There were three squadrons at the base and each one was virtually autonomous in the way it worked. There were two courses of up to twenty students at day one and there was a graduation on the last Friday of every month with a new intake arriving the following Monday. But it was a tough trial for anyone. Officer training lasted sixteen weeks and at the end of that time, for a very brief period, there was a feeling that perhaps you had made it. Very soon I came to realise I had barely scratched the surface. When it came to the standard that was required, you simply could not be good enough.

Every time I thought I had made the grade there would be a new hurdle to overcome. Perhaps the very best example of how tough it was would be that the senior course on my squadron – number 33 – had only three students left by the time I arrived and only one – a New Zealander called Colin Stagg – actually gained his wings. What a passing out parade that must have been!

I came into contact again with Colin many years later at Greenclose Aviation in Bournemouth, one of the instrument flying training schools I had considered as I made my transition from military to civilian flying. It was then

I came to appreciate that Colin had only recently decided to forgive me for borrowing his pride and joy – a Ford Cortina 1600E – only to put it into a ditch after hitting two unsuspecting pheasants at rather high speed all of twenty years earlier. It was just a phone call but he made me promise to share a bottle of fine Irish whisky with him purchased at my expense so that I could provide a full explanation of what exactly had happened that evening on a winding Yorkshire country lane. We still have to sink that bottle . . .

When I first arrived at Linton I wasn't particularly fazed by the set-up. The base in many respects was 'standard Nato'. I knew what an officers' mess looked like because I had just spent four months in officer training. The layout of an airfield was familiar to me. I had done my gliding training at RAF Cosford and air experience flying at RAF Shawbury and they were pretty much the same. If you'd seen one you'd seen 'em all. They were all among hundreds built in the late thirties and early forties; a typical three-runway affair laid out in a triangle. Even now Linton has the stamp of the pre-Second World War layout.

In the days when Neville Chamberlain was Prime Minister, any piece of land designated by the Air Ministry was transformed into an airfield inside six weeks. Now, as I fly over East Anglia in my civilian aircraft, I always look out at the remains of so many airfields that were hurriedly built before and during the last war. A great many of them were rendered derelict before they were even completed. Those days of military aviation were so intense that every flat piece of land along the eastern side of England was instantly covered in yards of concrete, such was the war effort. As I look back I realise the enormity of the machinery that was set in motion to sustain a war that lasted – not six weeks like the Gulf War – but almost six years.

But by the seventies there was a refreshing newness to Linton.

I was quickly learning codes of behaviour from a new standpoint. Now, if an airman broke a window he could face a few days in the cooler for vandalism. As an officer, if I broke a window I would be expected to pay double the cost and offer everyone a round of drinks. My behaviour was put down simply to high jinks.

It was like learning a new language where the words took on new meanings. I soon found myself doing and saying the same things I had seen in films that once I would have laughed at. Now I said things like 'wizard' and 'tally ho' – they had become part of my new culture. Each one of us from the outside was seen to be a typical RAF officer. We were loud and brash and very conceited. We lived for the day because even at such an early stage of our careers we recognised that we were being trained to the limit. One false move meant a guaranteed appointment with the grim reaper and the rest of the guys would drink on your bar book until it was removed by the accounts department and the taxpayer footed the bill.

Many of the shops, pubs and clubs in nearby York would accept your mess bar number to settle an account. By the tenth of the following month we would sign a cheque payable to the president of the mess committee to pay off outstanding debts. I remember once reading in a translated Russian propaganda document that the average Royal Air Force officer was certainly an aristocrat and therefore a 'bit of a pansy'. It claimed the salary we were being paid by the government would not keep us in perfume and silk gloves. What amused me was that my mess bill every month very often exceeded my salary.

Those days at Linton definitely symbolised a milestone for me. It was a crossing over from an ordinary middle-class background that I had left behind to the upper echelons of privileged officer society. A typical example of this transition was my relationship with my future father-in-law for whom I had always had the utmost respect and affection. He had been a company sergeant major in the Grenadier Guards and had served with distinction in the North African and Italian campaigns during the Second World War.

He'd always been proud of his wartime military career, but when I became an RAF officer his attitude towards me changed. There was a new respect, not one I was sure I deserved but it was one that he gave without being aware of it. Our relationship shifted by the very fact that I was a commissioned officer in Her Majesty's Forces while he remained in the ranks. He came to my Wings parade at Linton and I know he was extremely proud of me, his future son-in-law. But there was a new distance between us, one of officers and other ranks.

RAF Linton still had its own legacy of the Empire, of two world wars and of victory and defeat. As a nation Britain had enjoyed a whole century on the side of the victors but at Linton there were some individuals who knew too well the sense of a crushing defeat. There were a handful of former Polish Air Force Officers whom at fifty-five years of age or older were reduced to sweeping around the parade grounds and the concrete paths of the officers' mess. I know for a fact that at least two of them had been master pilots.

There was one refugee who, as we walked by in our

number one uniforms, would turn his broom into a rifle as he stood upright with his right arm drawn across his chest in a salute. The road sweeper came to life in our presence but as soon as we had passed he returned to sweeping duties, alone with his memories of the past.

Some weeks after I arrived at the base I found an old warrant officer uniform which I asked the old sweeper to wear while he gave us drill instruction. He agreed to both requests and later that day he greeted us with 'Good evening, gentlemen,' then he had a dozen of us drilling up and down an empty hangar to perfection. I noticed that he had pinned on his chest his own row of three medals. The two I picked out were the Distinguished Conduct Medal and the Military Medal. He saw me looking at these and as our impromptu drill practice came to a close he came over and quietly spoke to me. He said 'Sir, the uniform may be yours but the medals are mine.' Days later I saw him again back at work, sweeping the roads around the stores building.

When I arrived for my training I was still a person with my own thoughts and will. But within three weeks I had been reduced to a quivering mess. It was exacting and demanding. There were many times when I believed I would never be good enough but I never for one moment thought of giving up. The salary was a shock to the system too. In civilian work I had earned as much as £18.50 a day at heavy engineering firms around Birmingham. My first pay in the Air Force was £4.15 a day.

But the change in my lifestyle was incredible. I had entered a new world. I had done nothing but look forward to joining number 36 course. The joining instructions had been on the study desk in my bedroom at home and I had read them time and again. It seemed we were expected to spend an hour at drill every morning before going back to our rooms to change for breakfast.

There had apparently been some problem with the standard issue black flying boots we all received on arrival. Some of the other flying crews had complained that they were too stiff. So, we were ordered to turn up at early morning drill in the same boots and PE kit. We formed up, a smart squad outside one of the hangars of A Squadron. A fierce flight sergeant drilled us for about twenty minutes. Then we had to run around the hangar six times in order to improve our physical fitness ready for flying training. Most of the guys were physically sick at the end of this ordeal, including myself.

Finally we had to march back as a squad along a detailed route back to the officers' mess. En route, we passed the airmen's mess and the senior NCO's mess in our PE kit and flying boots. It was embarrassing to say the least. As we rounded the corner to the front of the officers' mess to take breakfast all was revealed to us. That particularly nasty flight sergeant was no more than a student on a course ahead of ours. The station photographer who had taken plenty of photo-graphs of us from a discreet distance made sure they were plastered all over the base. He was one of the flying instructors. The whole thing had been a very well-planned and well-executed spoof and we were a group of complete donkeys.

But now it was time for the real work, although for weeks later, whenever we were introduced to some new member of the staff, we would be suspicious and wonder whether or not they were really a squadron leader or flight commander or just a cleaner or the cook.

During the first six weeks until the end of February

1974, the routine was rigorous. Much of the day, starting at about 8.30a.m. until about 5p.m. was taken up with studies: physics, aeronautics, meteorology, the engineering of the Jet Provost and of course the regular reinforcement training of how to be not only a jet pilot but also an RAF officer. Regular sporting events and competitions took place too.

The general service training officer had no neck, his hair was about a quarter of an inch long on his head and he looked more like an all-in wrestler than an RAF officer. But his two daughters were quite gorgeous and regular targets for the new recruits out on nocturnal exercise . . . His aim was to continue our officer training from the Henlow days. He was a very hard taskmaster and made us work. At the end of the working day it was back to your room for a couple of hours further study.

I was very lazy and academically I produced results just good enough to scrape through. But when we took some mock exams after about six months on the course my results were pretty close to appalling. The station commander took a personal interest in my progress and I was called along to his office for an interview. His name was Group Captain Banard and he was known to nearly everyone as Barn Yard. He informed me that the only way he could see that I would come up with the necessary academic goods was to go along to his own home on the base each evening for an hour's private study. I went along to his house and I worked. He was the friend who introduced me to the wonders of meteorology – a passion I have had from then until now.

I am still fascinated by the weather and I thank Group Captain Banard because he helped me to understand it almost as well as the experts. I also went from bottom of the class to join those at the top; in fact I ended up on that course as second overall. It was quite a considerable transformation.

I took my first flight in an RAF jet as a trainee pilot on 26 February 1974. The instructor was Flight Lieutenant John Day and it was one of those lovely crisp, spring mornings. There was frost on the ground and very light frost on the aircraft and a feeling that you could see for a million miles. I took ages strapping in even though I had practised the art whenever I could sneak into a deserted hangar.

Suddenly we were off and forty minutes later we landed and I was rebriefed to fly a further hour-long sortie that day. It was just fantastic. There is no real way to describe the experience – you just have to be there. The joy of flight is so totally unique. Years on, I only have to look at someone who flies to know that they too have felt the same buzz of excitement.

Training continued through February into early March with each of the exercises getting slightly more difficult and demanding. Medium turns and then steeper turns, learning how to regain control of an aircraft of which you had lost control. Flying approach to landing and takeoff. Finally on 14 March 1974, a few weeks after I had first set foot in an RAF aircraft I was completing my first solo flight at RAF Elvington.

The airfield had an incredibly long runway near to Linton and was where they sent the trainees on their first solo. One of those runways was very difficult to miss and if you really did cock things up you could almost land across it as well as along it. It was a time when most of us were ready to sample a solo flight. Our instructors nervously sat in the control tower as we fledgling pilots were let off the leash.

It was another milestone on the way to becoming an RAF pilot. I look back with a great fondness to my flying training days and I know that much of the pomp and ceremony that I had once enjoyed no longer exists. The officers' mess at Linton-on-Ouse was typical of its day. The mess was in the shape of an H with the centre consisting of an administrative area. The officers' mess had a day room full of beautiful leather armchairs and there was an exquisite dining room.

At each end of the H there were two-storey buildings comprising private rooms for the officers. One senior member of staff once described to me the difference between the officer recruits from Henlow and the few who joined as graduates. He said that the university recruits would never be seen to pick their noses in public but that all officers pissed in their washbasins.

The bar at Linton was a fabulous place. At this early stage in my flying career it was time to listen to the flying stories of the experienced. But before very long we had our own 'war' stories to tell over a pint in the bar.

My batman George was an absolute gem. His position has long since been outmoded in the new and updated RAF. By the time I joined the Air Force I had to share him with three or four other officers. George was about 470 years old with an awful stoop. But when he had been at my uniform for an hour or so you could cut butter with the creases in my trousers and comb your hair in the shine on your shoes. He was completely unflappable and handled his little band of young men with great skill. For this work he was awarded on top of his fairly meagre wages, £1 a month paid by each one of his charges.

Before we graduated from Linton with our Wings, George the batman was found dead in Steve Thorne's room. It was a sad moment and we sent fitting tributes to his family. But I can't imagine old George wanting anything more than to die of a heart attack toiling at the job he loved. He had lived and breathed for his young officers as he turned them out to serve in the RAF.

During my time at Linton I managed to get through three cars, including the TR-5 which I arrived in. Then there was a two-seater Lotus Europa followed by a Lotus Elan Plus Two. I drove each of those cars to the limit down every country lane as fast as I could tearing the guts out of the engine. It seemed to me even then that I was living a privileged and charmed life.

Each weekend I vowed not to sleep but to get as much action out of the time as I possibly could. One Sunday morning, at about 4 or 5a.m. I was driving back up the A1, not very far from Ripon, when I simply fell asleep at the wheel. Looking at the tyre marks after I had crossed the central reservation of the dual carriageway for about 500 yards, it appeared I had come back to the other side of the road between the two uprights of a motorway sign. At this stage I had woken up, put my foot hard on the brakes and spun the car, bouncing backwards off the dual carriageway and through a five-bar gate into a field. The back of the car was a bit cracked and I had lost an oil filler cap. My pride had been dented but there was no other damage. In the end a police car arrived to pull me out of the ditch as I explained that I had lost control having swerved to avoid a rabbit.

There was another occasion, once again on the Great North Road, when three of us were travelling in three soft-top vehicles, each with the hood down. Each car had about three or four occupants. We were off on our way to yet another three-day course in our training. It was very early on a crisp spring-like morning when it was unlikely there would be anyone else on the road. It still sends shivers down my spine to think of what we did, but we were all young budding fighter pilots and it was the thing to do.

Our three sports cars were travelling at about 80mph along the A1 in a V formation no more than five or six inches apart from each other. But to have been in a V meant you were expected to have occupied a seat in each of the three cars. So at that speed and arrangement we all rotated from one car to another. Thankfully the police were not around to witness that particular acrobatic display.

To be withdrawn from flying training in the Air Force was known as getting the chop. I think about a third of the students on my basic course at Linton were chopped. We started out with roughly thirty-six students and finished with about twenty-four. I think in the majority of cases those guys withdrawn from flying training were relieved because the demands being made on them – that they were not coping with – were finally removed. They would have known that their chances of making the grade were poor and in many cases impossible. But the system was almost clinically cruel in the way it dealt with those students who were withdrawn from training. There was a parallel with the days during the Battle of Britain when guys who didn't come back had their rooms cleaned and their personal effects removed almost as though they had never existed. Perhaps the official reason for doing that was so it would not undermine those who still remained.

In our case you could often tell when someone had

reached his own limit. Perhaps he wouldn't come down to be with the rest of his comrades for a meal or if he was eating in the dining room he preferred to sit alone. At times it was almost a case of 'now you see me, now you don't'. One or two of the guys who had come in like lions went out like lambs and several of the others fought very hard to be retained in training. They might, if they were very lucky, get a few hours extra training in the area they were finding particularly difficult or they might simply be chopped.

It was usually down to the chief instructor or his deputy to fly the final ride with the student concerned. It was was always known as 'the Chop Ride'. Many of the guys, knowing that this was probably the last time they would ever sit in a two-seat fighter trainer simply went up for an hour and a half's aerobatics with the chief flying instructor only to return and receive a rubber stamp declaring they were no longer required in flying training. Lots of the guys were given a second string and given the opportunity to go into a ground branch, and I met many of them in their ground jobs. I am not sure whether or not that was a good thing. I am sure the memories for them were disappointing if not painful and for me it was awkward.

I am as certain now as I ever was that if I had been finally and absolutely removed from flying in the RAF, there was no way I would have stayed on doing any other job other than being a pilot. Sometimes on the old chopping front there really were some surprises. There would be the typical arrogant spark who achieved all the right exam results and seemed to know everything even before he started. He'd be at home in the air, he had the sports car and the string of beauties hanging on to his every word. Then suddenly he would be gone. I had a next door room mate who to me showed all the qualities but maybe there was a little bit of sham or bravado. Then one day he was simply gone. His car was no longer in its parking slot, his room was as clean as a pin and smelled only of polish, waiting for the next occupant. I often wonder what happened to him.

I felt quite sorry for a lot of my fellow students in basic flying training who were chopped and I felt incredibly sorry for some of them. But, what I and they did not know was the tremendous grief which occurred over the years. It was not just those who lost their lives but those who were taken out of flying training at a very late stage, not within their first few months, as they reacted to the shock of new demands, but after more than two years of shedding blood and sweat and tears. When perhaps only weeks from joining a squadron, these individuals fell at the last hurdle. They were the ones to feel really sorry for.

I was taken off flying training during a Hunter refresher course. I managed to bluff my way onto helicopters and then even managed to wangle my way onto the front-line fighters in the RAF. Yet there were other blokes on my course who were much further through their training than me and were taken off their fast jet training or weapons conversion courses to be told they could not continue as pilots. Whether or not that was fair I just don't know.

There was a chap on my basic training course who was the first winner of all five prizes on the course; not just ground studies and officer qualities but also the flying prizes. He went much further than me in his training but was eventually chopped during weapons training to be told he could never continue as a pilot. Now he is a wing commander in the Air Force and a navigator – and I have to say that is something that I simply could not and would not have done. To have gone through pilot training and then spent my career at best hoping to sit in a two-seater aeroplane behind a guy who was doing the job that I would have given both arms and both legs to do would be impossible for me.

Yet I can understand why we lost so many pilots during those training days. While most of us had sharp enough reactions to perform an individual task, there were others who could not tolerate what is known as the load factor. The workload of the modern day fighter (i.e. its capabilities and therefore the demands placed on its pilot) is incredible in that it is very high by comparison. It is worth mentioning that the joystick on the Tornado fighter bomber has eight separate functions. When flying a Tornado in combat it is the hands and eyes that do all the work.

At the time all I ever wanted to do was be a Lightning fighter pilot and I wasn't prepared to consider anything else. Even the pay didn't matter. I was here to learn how to fly a Jet Provost. The aircraft is described as a derivative of the Hunting Percival Provost which had been developed in the late forties as a military trainer. Initially it had a big Alvis rotary engine and propeller at the front. By the time I was training the petrol engine had been taken off the front and replaced by a Rolls-Royce Viper jet engine positioned behind the two pilots who sat side by side.

The early Jet Provost models could fly at around 250mph and the later versions could achieve 300mph. At the time I thought this was supersonic – I'd only ever flown aircraft like a Cessna 150 doing a top speed of around 90mph. Now I was learning to fly a machine easily capable of covering five miles a minute or a mile in twelve seconds. I had always thought that half the speed of a fired bullet was quite enough. Soon I would be flying half as fast again. Within months I'd be flying solo, flying faster than the speed of sound – it was fantastic!

The aircraft was a low wing monoplane of metal construction with a retractable undercarriage and a single jet engine – the RR Viper – with eight stages to the compressor. In essence it was a very simple aeroplane, ideally suited to a training role. Above all, it was very forgiving. A jet engine, while obviously very complicated to an engineer, is in fact amazingly straightforward and reliable when it is actually functioning. It still uses the same principle today – a basic internal combustion four-stroke engine: induction, compression, ignition and exhaust. Or for simpletons like us, struggling to grasp with the rudiments of mechanics: suck, squeeze, bang and puff.

The first time you look into the cockpit of any aeroplane, the whole thing seems a daunting array of switches, dials and lights. It soon becomes clear as to why you received such a vigorous eye colour blindness test during the medical – the cockpit is a complete spectrum of different coloured lights. Immediately in front of the pilot is the flying instrument panel giving the pilot precise information as to his situation during flight.

There are six instruments arranged in two horizontal rows of three and that basic panel layout has not changed since the earliest powered planes like the Spitfire needed instruments. The top left of these instruments is an air speed indicator known as ASI, calibrated in nautical rather than statute or road miles per hour. And the top right-hand instrument is the altimeter. The top centre instrument is the artificial horizon whereby the glass panel on the front of the instrument is etched with a gold wing to symbolise the aircraft. Behind that is a gyroscope that shows earth and sky divided into brown and blue. So when the aircraft is sitting on the ground, the symbol would split the colours on the instrument; one wing high or low would indicate a turn and the whole aircraft symbol covering brown or blue would indicate climbing or descending flight. Centrally, that is the most crucial instrument on the aircraft.

In the weeks leading up to the first sortie we'd burned the midnight oil learning and relearning what seemed like an endless set of checks. The checklist looked rather like a secretary's shorthand notepad. You could flip over to check the instructions that had to be learned by heart. We used little mnemonics to help us to remember the checks. One was Welshman for pre-takeoff – the check code being TAFFIO HHHCP.

At this early stage I hadn't developed the skill of putting any of the checks to the back of my mind. It was a constant cramming exercise in the weeks leading up to that first flight. I remember a crisp February morning in 1974, in fact it was the 26th, when Flight Lieutenant Day and I walked out to our aircraft. I was wearing my brand-new green flying suit. It smelled of mothballs as it had only just come out of the stores.

Trip one was called familiarisation. I must sit back and relax before I tried to carry out as many of the prestart exercises I could. This time the instructor was there to help me out. The flying was just a once around the block – or in our case the city of York. I returned to base with a mixture of feelings. I was on the road to becoming a pilot but I was so confused and overwhelmed by the array of detail and flying paraphernalia that I knew I must learn in order to see it through. I watched Flight Lieutenant Day's hands moving around the cockpit with such precision and confidence – like a magician performing a trick – as he first possessed the aircraft and then persuaded it to fly.

I flew again that day and after being briefly shown the effects of the controls it was my task to fly the aircraft in straight and level flight. With the instructor in charge it had earlier been a smooth ride. But the minute I took over it was like being on a switchback ride and everything went terribly out of control. In minutes my instructor was in charge again and everything went back to being straight and level. Then it is my turn once more and we are off again on this roller coaster ride diving straight off the rails as I wrestled with the aircraft. But each time I managed to inch towards a better control of the aeroplane as everything began to click into place.

I already had my private pilot's licence which I had earned through my flying scholarship – but this was very different and three times faster than anything I had known before. I knew I had to take the whole thing in my stride because compared to the machines I one day hoped to fly, this was a mere toy. Each of those lessons lasted about an hour and we were programmed to fly twice a day but the meticulous briefing and debriefing that packaged each flight easily added two more hours to the exercise.

One of the first rumours that I needed to dispel from my head is that you must have no fear of heights in order to become a good pilot. A good few flyers I know are simply terrified of heights. One used to close his eyes as he climbed up the ladder to his aircraft and at home he could not even stand on a chair to change a lightbulb. I know that particular pilot went on to fly Lightnings. In fact I have found as I have grown older that I am not keen on heights anymore. If I ascend a tower I can sense a fear in the pit of my stomach as I lean over the rail to view the earth below. But the difference is that being high above the world in an aircraft conveys a marvellous feeling of detachment and control over the world below rather than any idea, however remote, of falling to the ground.

Up in the sky I have always felt a warm, fuzzy feeling, almost a smugness at the thought of controlling so much power in my hands. As I progressed through my training I developed skills I had only dreamed of. If I felt like looking at the earth from a different angle I only had to invert the aeroplane. I began to feel that I had the power almost to turn the world upside-down while my aeroplane remained in the same position.

Aerobatics is an exciting and demanding skill. There is the G-force; the physical punishment that your body takes. When you pull on G you blackout. The corsets we all wear in fast jets help to increase the body's tolerance. Your eyes are so full of blood that when it is forced to leave your eyes as you ascend you can no longer see. The eyes have been 'blacked out'. At first it is as though you are looking through a pair of kitchen rolls, all peripheral vision has gone. It is like the action of a camera shutter closing over your eyes. In the end there is only a pinpoint of light left and then nothing.

The opposite of blackout is redout. Instead of experiencing positive G-force as the aircraft ascends at high speed it becomes negative as you descend again. Instead of all the blood rushing out of your toes it does the opposite and rushes out of the top of your head. In those early days you could always spot someone who had been performing a few aerobatics a little too hard. He would have bright red eyes that were extremely sore – a sure sign of too much blood in the eyes.

In the early days I never believed that I would eventually

regard the mechanics of flying as second nature. But I made that transition to learn to fly an aeroplane as a matter of course.

Despite the demands of training there was still time for young officers to indulge in extra-curricular activities of our own making. We held contests and competitions that brought some light relief to the serious stuff of the day. The Grimmy competition was the very worst contest of all. One that took place in midsummer of 1974 was the worst of them all. We were well through the basic elements of Jet Provost flying training and were getting into the much more interesting phase of aerobatics and formation flying. This was the real technique of becoming one with the machine before going on to more advanced skills.

York had one or two very advanced nightclubs to my recollection, and one of the games we used to play was to see who could find the ugliest woman to bring along to the officers' mess bar and this was known as the Grimmy competition.

It was a Saturday evening in the bar and a dozen or so of us had decided to stay around, either to do a little more study, polish the car or simply to relax. It was decided that we would have a Grimmy competition and individually or in pairs we jumped into our cars and roared off into York. I was with Nick Saunders. I parked my Lotus outside a York club and in we went for a couple of drinks and a few dances.

It's embarrassing to think about it now but I saw this young lady and she was a star – she looked like a bumble bee in a black and yellow hooped dress. She was short and squat with frizzy hair and lots of spots. I suggested we should go back to my club to round the evening off.

She saw the car outside and was smitten, not suspecting a thing.

The rule was that you had to be back in the bar by midnight complete with your Grimmy. I opened the door of the bar and walked in. Everyone had done very well that evening. There were some of the plainest and ugliest women that you could wish to see. My partner for the evening, Gloria, took one look around the room and realised what was happening and then promptly burst into tears. She was joined by most of the women there. It took a couple of minutes to grab my thoughts together before I realised what a heel I had been and I think most of us were shifting from foot to foot to try and play down the embarrassment we all felt.

I stood up on a table telling everyone to hush as I simply explained that we had not so far demonstrated our skills at being gentlemen and that it had been a foul and inexcusable trick to play. I added that the least we could do was to offer our guests proper hospitality. If they wished to stay we could book them into rooms in the mess and the following day we would organise a car ride out into the Yorkshire Dales where we could enjoy a pub lunch and a jolly day out. In fact it turned out to be a really pleasant evening and we were all forgiven for the high jinks that had earlier been so very insulting to our female guests.

There was also a prize during the course of our training to be given to the young officer who brought along the worst apparition of ugliness to a social event. When the particular officer I can recall was presented with his prize, he embarrassingly shuffled away. We later discovered that his guest was also his wife!

Some of the pubs on the moors and in the Dales of

North Yorkshire are among the loveliest I have ever visited. We used to go out, either with our sweethearts or en masse, especially for a fairly heavy-duty Sunday lunchtime session. Sometimes the landlords would look upon us as a blessing but I think there were other occasions when our arrival was decidedly unwelcome. Invariably the latter were always rewarded with either a preamble or a legacy.

The preamble was someone on a low level navigational exercise who would find a likely looking spot to mark on his map having overflown the pub a couple of times before flying back to base to tell us all about it. But it was more likely that if we had stumbled across a pub for a Sunday lunchtime we would return in the next day or so to overfly the place, always a little lower and faster than the aviation regulations allowed. It was our way of saying a 'Thank you' for putting up with us. Most of the publicans would come out to wave us on our way; they knew we had been the lads propping up the bar for the best part of the previous Sunday.

My first introduction to survival training came during basic flying training at Linton. I went on to become a survival instructor in the RAF having completed a series of training courses. It is amusing to me that the only course I did not go on, because the RAF had cancelled it, was desert survival. Yet when my time came to go to war the only survival I needed to have trained for was the desert.

At Linton it was widely acknowledged that the week's survival course from basic training was extremely demanding and it was the toughest test anyone would be willing to endure during peacetime. In simple terms it was simulated that you had ejected from your Jet Provost and would have to spend up to a week surviving on the bleak Yorkshire moors.

It seemed to me that first of all it was an incredible waste of money in that you actually went out to survive in flying kit that you had been issued with. Heavily padded and very expensive jackets and trousers came back at the end of the week absolutely wrecked, only to be replaced by brand new equipment for every man. Additionally, you were issued with a parachute which had been time expired although it appeared to have absolutely nothing wrong with it. This thing would be cut up into pieces to make an individual tent and sleeping bag. Much of the parachute webbing would be discarded and the rest with the parachute container would be transformed into a makeshift haversack.

But the survival week was very difficult. We walked between twenty and thirty miles a day which meant at the end of the six days you had covered not far short of a couple of hundred miles. No food was issued and the only luxury we were allowed was ten cigarettes if you were a smoker. I got through mine in the first couple of hours.

If you failed the course or pulled out for some reason, then it was back to base for a brief recuperation before starting again from scratch. I remember a couple of chaps who only passed at the third attempt, the poor sods. I have never before or since seen my own feet or anyone else's so badly blistered from the amount of walking we did. At the end of the week we all returned to base fairly cut about and bruised. It was not an experience I would like to repeat. About five or six years on I did some survival training with the Special Air Service Regiment. It may sound rather unlikely but I honestly don't think that training was as challenging as the one I had endured on basic flying.

There was never a problem getting water during the week. We took containers with us to dip into local streams and we were supplied with purification tablets. But food of course was a problem, especially as we had used up a considerable amount of energy while covering so many miles. On about day six we were given a live chicken to share between two or three. It was amusing to see how attitudes change towards other living creatures when you are all starving hungry. I was one of those who just wanted to rip the thing to pieces and cook it there and then. But there were others who simply couldn't face the prospect of killing something to then eat it. However, the chicken was always duly dispatched to be cooked over an open fire. Just a few mouthfuls each was enough to dramatically restore our spirits.

A particular sting in the tail of the survival course came as we thought we were coming close to completion. As we walked over the brow of a hill, there at the bottom was a coach with a couple of our instructors standing outside it. We trotted off down the hill simply delighted that at last it was all over. At the back of the coach was a tableful of cartons of milk. We got to within about fifty yards of the coach when the instructors cruelly folded up the table, putting the cartons of milk back into the coach before driving off. All that was left was a blackboard with some grid references chalked on which meant we had about another eighteen or twenty miles to do and it was unlikely that the exercise would be over at least until the following morning. Of course the first reaction was to just sit down there feeling utterly desolate and despondent. Right then, our instructors were all the bastards in the world. But you go one of two ways. There is a mixture of resentment and defiance that wills you to go on and to complete the course. Or a feeling that you have been beaten and cannot find the willpower to fight on. Luckily for us, with a little rallying around to beef up the team spirit we were off again. The next time we saw that bus we did indeed clamber aboard. It was all over.

The amusing end is that when you get back to the officers' mess and after a quick shower and shave before breakfast, there were some whose stomachs had shrunk so much through lack of food that just one mouthful of a sausage had them throwing up. But I can remember ordering a fried English breakfast twice. It arrived on a couple of dustbin-lid-sized plates and I duly polished the lot off. The only relaxation of the dress regulations over the next few days was that we were allowed to wear carpet slippers over our very sore and heavily blistered feet. The trick was to burst the blisters with a needle and wash your feet in methylated spirits. It made your feet sting like mad but it hardened them off in no time at all.

When I'd applied to the Air Force the first time I was asked if I would be prepared to consider any other aspects of the RAF if my flying ambitions were unsuccessful. I replied that I wouldn't and I am glad that I stood by that because one of the options later offered to me was a job as a flight line mechanic. The reason given for this was that I would be working very closely with aeroplanes, I'd have a lot of responsibility and could look forward to promotion at an early stage.

While at Linton I became as friendly as you could with one of the men who looked after the very basic maintenance of the jets. He was known as Tiny and he had a Higher National Diploma in engineering which is almost a degree qualification. He was certainly a bit rough around the edges but he deserved to be valued as something more than a petrol forecourt attendant which, as I soon discovered, was all a flight line mechanic ever was. The most responsibility these guys ever got was to put aviation fuel into the tanks of the jets. Other tasks involved cleaning windscreens and pumping up tyres.

Naturally poor old Tiny, who had signed on for nine years, was counting the days to when he could leave the service. He resented the Air Force bitterly and I can fully appreciate why. Still, some recruiting officer somewhere had done his job and filled his quota.

Prince Hamad Al Thani was a student on my course. He was a good pilot and I believe that he is now Commander in Chief of his own Air Force in Quatar. But at the time he was just one of the students, although there were obviously some distinctions. He never drank but he loved to come into the bar and share a joke with the boys. His favourite tipple was orange juice, no ice or lemon. During the survival exercise, when we had killed the chicken, he couldn't eat it because it had not been slaughtered according to the rules of Halal, strictly laid down in the Koran, the Moslem's holy book.

Once an airman broke into his room where Prince Hamad kept dozens of his tailor-made suits. When the Prince was asked if anything had been taken, he said he felt that it was just a little loose change from the pockets of his suits. But after the airman was caught and searched it was discovered that he had almost £1000 of Prince Hamad's money on him.

One Friday evening when my car was in the dock following another country lane scrape, the Prince brought his car round to the front of the officers' mess and gave me a lift home which was 150 miles away. When we arrived in the West Midlands he wouldn't even come in for a cup of tea but he arrived to collect me on Sunday evening on the dot of 8p.m. to chauffeur me back to the officers' mess at Linton.

At our graduation and Wings parade Hamad's family flew into Linton in their private jet. I believed that it was something of a surprise that the correct flight plan for landing at a military airfield hadn't been filed. But we were perfect hosts to this Middle Eastern royalty who had just popped in to see a favourite son on his graduation day.

When I finally moved the following year to RAF Valley in North Wales with my young bride our address was 19 Penrhyn Close. The families' officer had already telephoned me at Linton to apologise about the place being in a bit of a state, as it had been empty for three months. He told us we would be eligible for a rent rebate to pay for the cleaning. But when Sheila and I marched into our new quarters we were scared to stand on the kitchen floor – it was absolutely spotless. You could have performed brain surgery on the kitchen table and even the garage was clean enough to sleep in.

Every room, apart from the kitchen and bathroom, had plush sage green carpets. There was a chesterfield three-piece suite in the sitting room and a beautiful walnut writing desk and bureau. At the time it was common knowledge among the married quarters that the only items missing would always be a can opener and a corkscrew. Being newly married we'd asked for our quarter to be fully furnished and it was – right down to the Wedgwood dinner service and a beautiful cut-glass punchbowl and silver ladle. Everything had a value which was dutifully kept on the inventory list for each quarter. Yet the crystal bowl was priced at just £7 and the solid silver ladle another £8. Needless to say, a couple of quarters later we 'lost' the set – and happily paid for it. The telephone had already been installed and was connected within minutes of the families' officer handing us keys to the front door.

There were some reminders of days gone by at Valley. Officers would still have their batting done for them if they were living in the mess. But in the years before any officer, whether he lived in the mess or with his wife and family in a quarter, would still have a batman turn up to press his uniform. Our first house – a three-bedroomed semi – still had the lightboard in the kitchen and scullery so the officer or his wife could summon the servant of the house.

There were other things about our quarter that I had not been used to at home. There was a downstairs loo which we never had. In fact almost as soon as we arrived I called my parents to tell them I was phoning from the downstairs lavatory.

All the quarters were beautifully maintained and I soon discovered that RAF quarters were the envy of the other services. But when the time came for a family to move on to another posting you virtually had to polish your way out of the front door. I have Brasso'd the pins of a plug and used cotton buds to clean the inside of keyholes. We had to take doorhandles off to clean behind them. When Sheila and I left Valley the female families' officer actually got down on her knees and put her head inside the toilet bowl to inspect under the rim with a dentist's mirror. And she told me to clean it again as she could see limescale on the porcelain!

The top came off the cistern to make sure that was clean too. I had already scrubbed the thing out with a Brillo pad.

But there were tricks to be learned. A hole from a picture hook in the wall could be disguised with toothpaste and food colouring. It would only take a warmish day for the new occupants to discover toothpaste dribbling down the walls . . . We were allowed to hang only so many pictures per room which kept the damage down, but we were charged fifty pence for each mark left on the wall.

On the inside of a window frame the putty that had become slightly discoloured through condensation had to be cleaned using scouring powder and a toothbrush. If your car had sprung an oil leak on the garage floor you would end up paying dearly for the mark. The answer was to use petrol and a scourer to scrub it off.

For the first few weeks of our life in married quarters we were almost too scared to use any of the kitchen implements. We had bought our own non-stick frying pan because we were reluctant to get the issue ones dirty. We wrapped them in old cloths and stored them away. But they had to be cleaned with Brasso before we finally marched out of the quarter.

At Valley I was dealt a terrible blow that could have put an early end to my flying career. I had graduated from the advanced jet course, in September of 1975, with an average assessment. However, there was to be a delay of at least four months before the next course of training could start at RAF Brawdy in South Wales. Instead of knuckling down to some serious skill consolidation, I organised some serious fun by arranging my attachment to an army headquarters in northern Germany. The fastest piece of military equipment I took control of was a Chieftain tank! I became pretty nifty at downing German beer too. By the time I returned to flying in February of 1976 it was as though I had never flown before. I had the reactions of a startled sloth and the co-ordination of a drunken octopus. Within a month I was withdrawn from RAF fast jet flying training. I was chopped! I was shattered but determined not to be beaten. One day at home alone I called a very senior officer at Valley, pretending to be an MOD official. To the officer I explained that young Pablo Mason was just the chap to transfer to Wessex Helicopters.

My next call was to the MOD – I already knew the appropriate department and had carefully checked the names of the movers and shakers there. My final call was to the boss of operations, putting him in the picture. It worked and in 1977 I was posted to fly the Wessex. I have banged out of aircraft and witnessed more than my fair share of near misses. But I felt then that I was the luckiest man alive.

4

72 Squadron, RAF Odiham – 1977 to 1980

Odiham is a typical thirties or forties RAF air base. The airfield is laid out in a triangle of three runways although two of them have long since ceased to be used. The main runway is a little over a mile long and runs roughly east – west. The runway numbers are 10–28. It is about five miles south-east of Basingstoke, south of the motorway running out of London and a reasonable hour from being able to sit in the RAF club with one's first gin and tonic. The officers' mess is typical, and in fact identical to so many dozens of officers' mess built in the late thirties and early forties.

Much of the station's history is shrouded in secrecy. During the Second World War quite a lot of the secret operations involving the transportation of spies was carried out from Odiham in the good old Lysander. Just before the Second World War broke out, the Royal Air Force was reviewed there by the then head of the Luftwaffe, Reich Marshall Goering.

After the war and well into the mid and late fifties it was a night fighter base. There was lots of evidence of that in Odiham village, particularly in the local pubs. I was disappointed to see that the Kings Arms which, the last time I went in there in the late seventies, had so many pictures and caricatures of the characters of the time with their night flying meteors, is now a Chinese restaurant.

However, back to the station when I knew it – 1977 to 1980. It was at that time devoted entirely to helicopter operations, although the occasional Hercules called in – one assumed to deliver equipment to surrounding army bases and of course the atomic weapons research establishment at Aldermaston needed some servicing. It was not an infrequent event for flying operations to be stopped completely while just one aircraft moved in and moved out. No degrees for guessing what was on board the aircraft.

Odiham was also home to 240 OCU (operational conversion unit) which was responsible for the conversion of crews to fly helicopters. At the time the helicopters on RAF inventory were the Wessex and the Puma.

At Odiham, 33 Squadron was a Puma squadron on the south side of the airfield, very much left to its own devices really, and 72 Squadron, the squadron that I was to join, with its Wessex lived in a hangar adjacent to 230 Squadron which also had Pumas. The Puma at the time was fairly new to RAF inventory. It was going through quite considerable teething troubles in terms of what it was allowed to do and what it was not allowed to do. We on the good old stalwarts, the Wessex, would enjoy tremendous amusement at the expense of Puma crews. The aircraft was known to all and sundry as the Stumbly.

I think it is fair to say that morale among the air crew of all of the squadrons when I arrived was particularly low. This was because of a number of factors. Most air crews were spending weeks, which turned into months, away from home either in Northern Ireland where the troubles were calling upon just about every able-bodied crew that was available and, of course, there were so many other commitments to the British Army of the Rhine and to the Ace Mobile Force. This meant that if you were not in Northern Ireland, the chances were you were in some European country. So there was the North Sea magnet, as it was affectionately known. The conversion from being a military helicopter pilot to a civilian helicopter pilot involved the expense of about £40 or £50 and a couple of exams in London, and then you could go and almost double your salary overnight in the oil fields while certainly improving your quality of life infinitely.

There were lots of PVRs which were requests for premature voluntary release from the service, and it was a source of great amusement because the wait for this release was anything up to five years and rarely less than three. One or two of the older guys on the squadron had their own reasons; someone called Stan Smith, who was in his mid-fifties, said he thought he would apply for PVR and that would mean that rather than retiring in a year's time, he would be not allowed to leave the service for anything up to another five years!

In fact the PVR scandal was relieved during my time at Odiham by a junior officer who went public – Flight Lieutenant Graham Wright. He wrote about his circumstances to the *Daily Telegraph* and there was a huge furore among the civilian population that people who desperately wanted to leave the Air Force, for whatever reason, were not being allowed to do so. These were people who had served out their time – they had done ten or fifteen years – and they just wanted to go a year or so before their sixteen year engagement was up. There were people who applied for PVR just as soon as they had finished their operational conversion training in order to be able to leave within three to five years and go out to the oil rigs. At the time it seemed as if there was no end to the demand for helicopter pilots in the North Sea and you could have almost written the salary you required rather than negotiate normal figures.

As for myself, I was just blissfully happy to have finally made it along the rocky road and to be flying helicopters, military helicopters. The thought never entered my head to want to go out to the rigs. There were a couple of ironies that I found quite amusing. One was happy hour – which Odiham was renowned for throughout the Air Force – starting at 5 o'clock on a Friday night and rarely ending before the early hours of Saturday – and we would get lots of ex-RAF pilots visiting from their bases from as far north as Stornaway or Aberdeen. These guys would pay £30 or £40 for a return air ticket to London and then a taxi ride between two or three of them from Gatwick or Heathrow to Odiham to spend a few hours in the officers' mess with their old comrades. It seemed to me that if life was so fantastic in the oil rigs and had been so abhorrent in the Air Force, what on earth were they doing spending a fair old whack of their weekly salary just coming back to join us in the pub? It also seemed to me that the guys delighted in telling us that they were now earning three-fold the salary they could hope for in the RAF but to them it never seemed enough. They always seemed to need that much more to make their lifestyles bearable.

In contrast at the time I didn't know anything about money. I was simply having a great time, money didn't matter and in any case there always seemed enough. To be doing the job I so loved seemed payment enough.

The officers' quarter that we were allocated was quite lovely – 5 Love Lane. A three-bedroomed semi-detached house – the carpets were new, the central heating was new and all efforts for energy saving, window sealing and double glazing, were installed during the first year of our occupation. It was such that if the faintest thing went wrong with any part of the house, a telephone call brought along the man from the Department of the Environment and it would be fixed in no time at all. It was as if no expense was spared to maintain the quarters. And what a tragedy it was when I visited friends there only five or ten years later to find that the quarters were in such a sorry state. It was something to do with an allocation of the budget when I was there and, knowing nothing whatever about it, there was money in a fund to be spent on quarters. But five years later there was not enough money in the fund but there was terrible waste as well. My friend who I was visiting told me about one house that had been struck by lightning. All that had happened was that two or three ridge tiles had been dislodged. If these had been replaced within a matter of days or perhaps even weeks then the damage would have been absolutely minimal and the cost relatively small. And yet the ridge tiles, he told me, had been left for something over a year and it was quite obvious that the roof was rotting and in no time at all would need renewing completely. As it was an RAF-owned quarter, the occupants had not been allowed to carry out any work themselves.

My first squadron commander was Wing Commander Tony Salter, a lovely man who always had a ready smile for everyone although a bit of a reputation for saying '72 can do'. He seemed to be reluctant to refuse any task that the squadron was given. He was replaced after a couple of years in a routine changeover by Tony Ryles, who was quite a different kettle of fish. He certainly gave me a hard time, although I don't think I did very much to make his tenure easy. The ground liaison officer, Major Bing Corner, amused me – typical Army, absolutely glowing boots and wherever he was, in the corner of a muddy field or in his office there was always time for tea.

I was on 'C' Flight. My flight commander was Squadon Leader Jim Clarkson – a fascinating man. He was one of those people, unlike myself, who could make a whole paragraph out of two or three words. He said very little but you knew exactly what he meant. A hard task master but a very fair man. Jim Clarkson was my flight commander for about a year and he went on to other things. I think he had a ground tour somewhere, I am not sure, but I did hear that he found God at some stage.

Martin Gardiner took over from Jim Clarkson as my flight commander. He was a very pedantic man, very thorough and incredibly fair. One of the things that I found typical of all of those in charge of me in those early days was they seemed to work incredibly hard. And what is more, I suppose it is evolution over time or maybe it is just a development within myself, at that time there seemed to be a loyalty not just to their seniors but to the people for whom they were responsible. In my latter days in the service that downward loyalty seemed to dry up horribly. Ambition was all consuming and the drive to get to the top was the sole objective rather than the need to do a job properly by looking after the prime asset – the men.

Paul O'Brennan was the deputy flight commander and

in those days of helicopter management he probably had more control or as much control as the flight commander himself. Paul was a junior officer but what he said went. He was a super guy and he became a legend, although he died in his early thirties of a massive heart attack.

Throughout my time at Odiham I had Bunty. Bunty was my Old English sheepdog. When we arrived there she was just under a year old and stone deaf – which had been looked upon by all of us as a terrible affliction and disability. In the early stages when the breeder offered to take her back we were inclined to do that, but of course we only realised she was deaf after having her for two or three months and when the breeder would not say what he was going to do to her, there was no way that she was leaving us. Anyway her deafness turned out to be an absolute boon. As she was stone deaf she could not hear even the highest of tones associated with dog whistles or the like and therefore initially she very discreetly came flying with me. When I realised that just about everyone, certainly on the station and probably throughout the support helicopter force, knew that she came flying then I kept her own flying log book. She must have totalled 600 hours flying with me in the Wessex and loved every minute.

One of the things that so many people noticed about Bunty was that she never barked unless we were flying over Basingstoke on our way home. I was not able to explain it then and I cannot explain it now. She would simply sit quite quietly in the back of the helicopter – if we had troops on board she would go and get a fuss from them – and yet when we approached Odiham within about four or five miles and certainly when we got anywhere near Basingstoke she would just put her muzzle though the crack in the main cargo door and bark her head off until we were back at Odiham. It would not matter if we had been on a task for just forty-five minutes or maybe been in Northern Ireland for two or three months.

Bunty had pups in early 1980, just before we left for Hong Kong.

She had ten of them, although one died soon after it was born. The whole station rallied round to assist in the upbringing of Bunty's pups. Rather than a whelping box I simply cut a door in half and nailed it across the access to the kitchen and that was the pups whelping box for the first six weeks with a lorry load of newspaper every other day to keep the place clean. Even the station commander and his children came along regularly with their tied-up bundles of paper just to look at and play with the puppies for half an hour or so. In fact, if we had not been going to Hong Kong I would almost swear that I would have been the proud owner of ten Old English sheepdogs, including Bunty, from then on.

There were several other fairly famous dogs throughout the Support Helicopter Force. Notably there was Oscar, a black crossbreed who belonged to Tony Jones. He was one of the pilots at Standards; that was where the super pilots went and made sure that everyone else was up to scratch. Oscar was more like a human being than a human being. Tony could tell him to go out to a particular aircraft on the pan and, I don't know if there was a code involved or not, Oscar would go out to that aircraft and sit and wait for his master. His obedience was absolutely unswerving, such that if Tony was flying a short trip of half an hour or so, particularly if it was an examining ride, he would tell Oscar to get in his box, which meant that he had to sit under a chair that Tony had pointed out to him and wait until Tony came back. Oscar would not move until Tony called him from his box.

One particular day a one-hour trip turned into a weekend trip as Tony was diverted from his task – he had to go out to Manston and then across to Belgium and he was away for a couple of days. No amount of coaxing could get Oscar to come out from under the chair, and I and another guy took him food and water over the weekend. He touched neither and just pined until his master returned. As soon as Tony greeted Oscar then Oscar was back to his old self – a quick fuss from his master and then a ravenous eating and drinking session until he was replete. Many of us wondered what would have happened if for whatever reason in the military world, Tony had not walked back through the door. I think Oscar would have just died where he lay.

My first flight on my first operational squadron was with Flight Lieutenant Chas Spinks on Friday 11 March 1977. Chas was a tall slim man who had seen it all before and done it a dozen times. He wore half-moon spectacles and looked rather like a schoolmaster, and that indeed was his manner – very calm and very collected and very quietly spoken. We flew around for about an hour and a half and he offered some points of advice but seemed reasonably satisfied with my performance and what I had learned on the Operation Conversation Unit. It seemed, however, that there was some urgency in my training and he told me that just as soon as they could they wanted me trained up and off to Northern Ireland. In a few days indeed, and that is precisely what happened. Conversion on the squadron should have taken about a month and a half but in fact it was all over bar the shouting within about a week.

Friday 1 April 1977 saw my first involvement in a real life Casevac – a casualty evacuation. Movement of casualties and accident victims by helicopter is almost commonplace today but in the late seventies it was the sole concern of Army and Air Force aviation – in fact on the UK mainland it was almost exclusively up to the Royal Air Force. I had been standing by as co-pilot to Bob Jones. We moved the casualty from Canterbury to Stoke Mandeville. The task had been on and off and on for days; we got to cockpit readiness, we even got the aircraft started up and just about airborne when we were told to shut down. It was either a case of the casualty not being ready to move or the weather being too turbulent to risk his life. In the event, on the morning of Friday 1 April we got the green light and rushed off to land at the county cricket ground of Kent at Canterbury. We landed in good time for the 9 o'clock meeting and touched down on the edge of the cricket circle. Bob was, and still is, a pilot for whom I have the utmost respect. I think he describes himself as vertically challenged which is quite true, he is certainly only a little bit over five feet tall, but what a pilot. I flew a lot with Bob in those early days and not just his skills of flying a helicopter stayed with me but the skills of being an airman and doing my job professionally. Bob left the Air Force and is now very successfully employed with Bristows Helicopters as their chief pilot.

The crewman for this particular operation was Master Air Loadmaster Keith Munday, known to all and sundry as King Rat. Keith could turn a dollar at just about anything – a good man for all that. A few years later Keith was commissioned and became an officer as an air loadmaster.

An ambulance drew up at the side of the helicopter and I made the mistake of looking out to see what was going on. A stretcher in a turning frame was drawn from the ambulance and therein amid this heap of body scaffolding was a young man in his early twenties, as white as snow, obviously in the most incredible pain. There were drips and bottles and monitoring machines all over the place and a couple of doctors and a nurse fussing about him. He was a young infantry private who had been involved in an Army exercise. He had been driving along in his soft-top Land Rover when something happened for the vehicle to go over – it had almost cut him in half. The doctor explained that his case was critical, that he had to get to Stoke Mandeville and movement by road was just impossible – it would kill him. We had to risk the helicopter journey because if he did not get to Stoke Mandeville he would die anyway.

Stoke Mandeville is just south-east of Aylesbury in Buckinghamshire and our route from Canterbury cricket ground was to take us right over the centre of London. Normally this would mean a few twists and turns over the city as we followed either the River Thames or the major highways. The idea behind this is simply that if the helicopter does suffer some kind of transmission failure then you can land on the best of the open spaces rather than the built-up areas. The routing would take us across paths and the major highways in order to give us the best chance to auto-rotate to a landing.

In this case things were to be different. Bob started up the helicopter and gingerly lifted us into the hover and from there we transitioned forwards into flight at a couple of thousand feet. He refused to use any of the stabilising equipment, he felt that he could fly the aircraft smoother than those pieces of kit could help us along. We took turns to fly for about ten minutes each. I hoped that the concentration that I was giving to the operation was mirrored in what I saw in Bob's face – complete focus on flying the aircraft as smoothly as we could. The doctor in attendance was on the intercom and as we approached Dartford he informed us that the patient was taking a turn for the worst. At exactly the same time the London controller told us to orbit in our present position until he could give us clearance to continue onwards towards Stoke Mandeville. As calmly as I could I advised the controller that any unnecessary or sudden movement of the aircraft would almost certainly result in the death of our patient. The controller was well aware that we were a Casevac aircraft because in these cases you had the call sign CASEVAC.

From then on life was magnificent. The controller was a total professional, instructions to us were clear and sharp: 'Maintain heading 304 degrees – future heading changes will be given as no more than five degrees and with at least two minutes' notice'. With the same authority he was telling airliners to overshoot and climb away from our path. We now had total priority to overfly London on our north-west heading towards Stoke Mandeville. And it seemed that all the big name airliners were being cast to the four winds. 'Dan-Air 421 climb to flight level 120, turn right onto heading 330, you are diverted to Manchester' and so on. We cleared London and ever so gently the controller turned us up to St Albans and Harpenden. Just as he promised he gave us gentle left turns and we were completely in his hands and just about as relaxed as we could be. Almost a shock, I was flying at the time when he told us to descend by about 500 or 600 feet. His final instructions were 'You are now on the final heading to land at Stoke Mandeville into wind. Stoke Mandeville is directly ahead of you by three miles. Look ahead and land. Good luck to you all.'

Bob took control of the aircraft and put us down just as gently as if he were landing this four tonnes of aluminium onto a table of raw eggs and not one of them would have cracked. The casualty was then lifted so gently from the aircraft.

Once again I looked down, a mistake I tried not to make on future occasions. The man was still in pain but he tried a smile as he looked up with obvious gratitude that he was being taken somewhere they could do the best for him and that we, as a small part of the chain, had done the very best that we could. When we got to Odiham later I telephoned the London Air Traffic Control. While the particular controller who helped us was no longer on duty I managed to track him down a few days later. He was like a dog with two tails – as he said, he had waited for an opportunity like that for a long time and thoroughly enjoyed it. We both agreed that the cost to the airlines must have been immense and equally agreed that no one would have complained about any part of the cost that they had had to bear. I also stayed in touch with Stoke Mandeville and in the event the casualty died about three days later.

The job of the military is principally to prepare for war, to support the government of the day in its endeavours and I suppose to act when the government of the day has failed with whatever it wanted to achieve politically. From a flying point of view, or more particularly from a helicopter flying point of view, in preparing for war and carrying out a number of exercises, our prime task was to support the Army. The main preparation was to exercise regularly and in different ways so that once every eighteen months or so you could take part in exercise TACEVAL – a tactical evaluation of your ability to fulfil your war role.

My first experience of a military exercise as an operational pilot was on Tuesday 5 April 1977. I was to fly, once again as co-pilot, but this time with Squadron Leader Noel Parker-Ashley – a charming and very dapper man who later went on to command a Puma squadron. He always had a ready smile and a certain easy manner about the way he got things done. What he also had was the most infuriating stutter and I have to admit that I found it mildly amusing when the operations staff gave him a call sign which made the most of his stutter. And yet as strange as it was, while he could rarely hold anyone's real attention in a conversation without having the greatest of difficulty in getting his words out, whenever he was in an airplane and on the radio transmitter his words flowed smoothly as indeed did his flying skills. The crewman once again was Keith Munday. At this early stage of the tender build-up of my flying skills I was only allowed to be with the best – the learning of bad habits would come later.

That morning at some ungodly hour of 3 or 4 o'clock, all the sirens went off accompanied by military vehicles driving round the station with their lights flashing and horns blaring determined to get the station on line just as quickly as we possibly could. The idea was that we had to be able to clear Odiham in no time at all. Naturally any potential enemy would know that it would be the centre of support helicopter operations for the Royal Air Force and it may well be an early target. Our job was to get just as far away from Odiham or to a deployment location as soon as we were released by the tasking authority.

As the sun started to rise we were given a deployment location. I quickly plotted it on our maps and we were quickly out to our aircraft and ready to go. Squadron Leader Parker-Ashley checked my plotting and confirmed that we were to go to a field very close to Royal Air Force Hullavington, which at the time was a parachute packing centre about six miles north of Chippenham in Wiltshire. I recall that the last time I had been there was something like ten years previously – we had been for a week when I was an air cadet for our annual summer camp.

I remarked to Squadron Leader Parker-Ashley that the orders were for us to depart Operation Tesseral. I did not know what that meant at all, but his eyes lit up, a broad smile covered his face, and he said that he would show me within the next few minutes precisely what it meant. We started up the aircraft and taxied out onto the airfield. King Rat had carefully loaded tents, machine guns, food and cookers, sleeping bags, tin hats and all the paraphernalia that would make us fairly autonomous apart from the need for fuel for anything up to a week ahead. Checks were completed in record time and the Squadron Leader taxied the aircraft along the runway and gently lifted it into the air.

I discovered within seconds that Operation Tesseral meant that we had to leave the station just as low and as fast as we could. It was a code word that indicated that aircraft leaving or arriving at the airfield may be the target of a close-in low-level missile attack and therefore our best means of defence was to stay just as low as we could so that no one would see us. I still remember it as one of the best roller coaster rides I had ever been on. For the first two or three minutes after taking off from Odiham I do not think the aircraft was ever more than ten or fifteen feet above the ground. The merest contour in the rolling fields was a route along which we could go. We followed the lines of streams and ditches. It was a technique that I used many times in the future. But on this particular occasion it had come as such a surprise, not to mention that we seemed to be flying along the streets of the married quarters and the local villages. It really was a very exhilarating way to go on my first day of practice war.

After the initial excitement we stuck to 1,000 feet or so and continued on our way to Hullavington. The precise grid reference we had been ordered to go to was in fact a small area of grass in between two hangars on the airfield at Hullavington. The hangars were the half-moon-type Nissen huts which in fact had turf on their roofs to make them that much more difficult to see from the air. Quite obviously they had not been used for years and it was the intention of the taskers that we should set up some form of camouflage between the hangars themselves. I was enjoying myself immensely and I was also all for making life just as easy as we possibly could even if that meant bending the rules slightly. Within ten minutes or so someone had found a set of strong bolt cutters, the padlock giving access to the hangars had been broken, doors were pushed open and our helicopter and the three others that joined us very shortly afterwards were pushed into the hangars. In time the communications boys arrived from somewhere and they set up long- and short-range comms from a makeshift office in the corner of the hangar. Then we had tea in lip-burning metal mugs which seemed to appear from just about everywhere. Just about as soon as the aircraft was inside the hangar with the door closed a message would come through for another task – a movement of troops or a movement of an undisclosed load from somewhere to somewhere so the aircraft would be out, warmed up and we would be off and flying it.

We lived in the hangar for about three days. I managed to rig up a cargo net in the roof of the Wessex and I slept quite comfortably in my sleeping bag there. Keith slept on the floor of the helicopter and Squadron Leader Parker-Ashley managed to sleep in one of the corner offices, after all he was in charge and did deserve something of whatever luxury we could find.

My officer training had taken firm root and the routine of getting up in the morning rarely differed even on exercise. We got up, washed and shaved which was an absolute priority, got a shine on the boots and made sure we were looking tidy and then if there was any time left at all you would have something to eat. That was where Keith was worth his weight in solid gold. He was one of the old stagers – a ready smile and a minute and a half would guarantee you would have a cup of steaming tea and bacon sandwich. Where they came from I never asked; I knew jolly well that if I did he would not tell me.

By that Friday evening we were all back at Odiham, tired but mostly in good spirits. Friday evening was always happy hour. I suppose in a heathen sort of way I have to admit that Friday night's happy hour while I was in the Air Force was as vital a ritual to me as any religious ceremony might be to the most pious of people. It was not unusual for me to be away for two or three months and to arrive home from exercise on the Thursday and yet be there in the pub at 5 o'clock on the following day. I do not know how Sheila, my wife, put up with this sometimes.

A MINEVAL exercise is generally organised and generated at station level and therefore those in the know had a good idea when they would take place. However, almost exactly one week after getting back from MINEVAL we were called out for TACEVAL (the tactical evaluation). There were some pretty long odds that the TACEVAL should take place when it did because it was the earliest possible date for it to happen and I think that most people were caught off guard. For my own part the exercise started a good deal differently than it did for many of my colleagues. All I remember is the telephone ringing at about 7 o'clock in the morning. I heard Sheila get out of bed, grumbling as she went downstairs that she had heard sirens and bells and lights flashing for hours and now who on earth was it phoning at this ungodly hour. I realised that I had missed the call out. By the time she had reached the bottom of the stairs and answered the phone I had got one leg into the trousers of my flying suit and was hopping round trying to get all my stuff together.

Squadron Leader Jim Clarkson simply could not believe that I had slept through all of the sirens and blaring horns as the house was no more than 100 yards from the station siren. If it had been any louder it would have taken the roof off. I cannot explain it and to this day that is the only call out I have ever missed. In the event I rushed into work, was bundled into a helicopter with its rotors turning and we went off to RAF Upavon which was our group headquarters out on Salisbury Plain. The exercise was just a call out and the object was to see how quickly the squadron could deploy to a field location. I think we went through with flying colours. At the time I was far too low in the pecking order to be anything other than a gofer. We were back home in time for tea.

Thursday 21 April 1977 saw my first deployment proper to Northern Ireland. I had been for the odd one or two days before this time but now I was there for a month and a half. Yet again I flew with Bob Jones and Keith Munday, and on our trip I remember we carried a VIP, Roy Mason, the Minister for Northern Ireland, from the airport at Aldergrove to Stormont Castle where he was going for a meeting of some sort. We waited for him for about an hour and then returned him to Aldergrove for his journey back to London.

The support helicopter world tended not to recognise weekends as any form of institution. From Monday to Friday we worked with the regular Army and the regular forces of the Navy and Air Force and at weekends we worked with the Territorials. I have to say that I very quickly realised that the weekend work was by far the most rewarding and often the most exciting. You were working with people who dedicated their spare time to being a part of the military, and also there was less civilian control because they were down to minimum mannings or indeed military control because the rest of the Air Force, particularly the swept and shiny fast jet fleet did very little on Saturdays and Sundays.

I had only been back from Northern Ireland for a few days when on the tasking board I saw a particularly interesting trip with Stu Mold and Howard Jones and I volunteered to go with them. We were working with the First Wessex Regiment, a Territorial outfit, which was quite appropriate because we were flying Wessex helicopters. It was fairly typical in those days for the accommodation available to Territorial units, particularly if they were working away from base, to be quite basic. And this particular exercise was taking place at Okehampton, a field training exercise in map reading on the north side of the moor itself. We were flying supplies of stores and food out to them actually on Dartmoor and we were also operating as a search and rescue if anything went wrong. But the accommodation was very basic and Stu Mould, quite rightly, refused it and so we got our little 'non-availability of accommodation suitable' chits signed and off we went to find a motel just outside of Okehampton. Having put the aircraft to bed and finished our day's work on Saturday we went off to the pub to round the day off with a few beers, probably a few too many because I do remember in the early hours of Sunday morning being fairly fully clothed in the motel swimming pool. There was I with Stu and Howard relaxing away the cares of the day when out came the motel owner shining his torch and making all sorts of noises that we should get out and go away until he realised that we were residents and then he apologised profusely and let us get on with our swim. We must have been making a helluva noise but fortunately it was fairly early in the season and so there weren't too many guests to annoy.

It was back home on Sunday evening to be back off first thing Monday morning for yet something else entirely new. Once again I was off as co-pilot to another pilot, this time Bob Best. Bob was a very well-respected helicopter aviator and he had been selected to fly the Wessex for Her Majesty's Silver Jubilee celebrations at RAF Finningley. Pete Dowell was the crewman, a young sergeant who had been in the Air Force about the same time as me and was known to all and sundry as Doris. We had to go to RAF Lindholme which is about six miles east-south-east of Doncaster and perform a precise exercise for Her Majesty, which involved towering in front of the royal dais at a height of about 200 feet and then deploying on a rope about half a dozen troops. We were staying at Lindholme because the mess at Finningley was full and I do recall the Monday evening being a very, very jolly occasion because of course the cream from all walks of the service had been brought in to carry out what was the first rehearsal prior to the Silver Jubilee celebrations later that year. Lindholme now I think is a prison.

By the middle of June 1977, some three months after joining 72 Squadron, I was well into tasking away from base on my own and I absolutely loved it. Quite regularly I could go to the various bases around the country where my friends in the fast jet force were still being given responsibility to do nothing other than make tea. I would land at the base, refuel, perhaps take them for a fly round for half an hour or so before continuing with whatever task it was that I had been set. On the weekend of Friday to Sunday the 10 to 12 June 1977 I was tasked to go up to the Otterburn training area in Northumberland for an exercise both with the First Battalion Junior Leaders Regiment and the First Battalion Parachute Regiment. My crewman was Bob Sutton who at the time was a sergeant, and he very much followed me through the military in that when I saw him several years later he had been commissioned and was a flying officer as a navigator of Tornadoes, although I never actually flew with Bob in the Tornado.

On the way up to Otterburn I chose to refuel at Leeming. I had a couple of friends there I was hoping to see and in the event did not manage it. But when I got to Leeming I was given the complete VIP treatment by the Officer Commanding Operations Wing at Leeming and this was because he thought that the squadron commander had telephoned him direct to say that I would be requiring an expeditious refuel on my way to my weekend exercise. In fact it had been nothing whatever to do with the squadron commander; it had simply been Senior Aircraftsman Brooks.

Brooks was one of the Air Force's out and out characters. He had been in the RAF for over twenty-two years and was still only an SAC. I assumed the squadron commander had anguished long and hard about whether or not to recommend him for promotion to corporal but felt that he simply could not do it. Brooks was an absolute charmer, he had the most delightful Oxford English accent and had in fact been educated at Eton. Unfortunately for him he had no commonsense whatsoever; a complete lack of a sense of priorities. It was a fairly fondly held joke that you could ask Brooks to walk your dog and take a top secret signal down to headquarters and then tell everyone to evacuate the building because it was on fire. And sure enough he would not tell anyone the building was on fire until he had walked the dog and taken the message down to headquarters.

He was a member of the local gliding school and quite a good pilot I was told. He also spent some time flying his family's light aircraft and everyone around thought that he was a wing commander and he gave them no indication he was anything else. He had no real respect or idea of rank. I think he felt that he wanted to go further in the Air Force but recognised that it was unlikely it was ever going to happen. Yet when he telephoned to book us accommodation or refuelling at other bases he would always act as though he was completely in command by just saying: 'Brooks here of 72 Squadron. I am sending one of my boys up to you – do try and look after him won't you?' and wing commanders and group captains

104

at the other end of the telephone would be saying 'Yes Sir, no Sir' oblivious to the fact that they were talking to a senior aircraftsman. To our knowledge Brooks was the only senior aircraftsman in the Air Force who held the Long Service and Good Conduct Medal with Clasp.

From Monday 27 to Thursday 30 June was my first ever Ranger. I continued to fly them throughout my Air Force career in various different aircraft. Basically a Ranger was a way of showing the flag. It was the opportunity to fly somewhere you rarely flew to both show that the Air Force was still in existence, to give the crews experience in going somewhere new and of course it was something of a jolly. It was one of those pleasant little opportunities to get an all-expenses few days away somewhere, and usually somewhere quite exciting. The civil servants hated us, but for some reason we could get the civil servants' allowance rates for wherever it was we went and rarely could you ever spend the allowance that was being paid to you.

My first Ranger was to Vaerlose in Copenhagen. We flew out from Odiham to Wildenrath in Germany to refuel and then north-bound up and across Denmark. I flew with Bas Longhurst and Clem Clements. I remember we had a fantastic time and it was a lovely journey up there taking four or five flying hours. Once our kit was deposited in quite a reasonable downtown hotel it was off first of all to the Tivoli Gardens. Tivoli is a large open-air space with fun fairs and other attractions to enjoy. Then we had a quick look around the town to get the 'culture stats' as we always use to call them – obviously a sneaky look at the girlie bars was included. The journey home was a far cry from the simplicity of the journey to Copenhagen in that the weather had really closed in and we had to fly through the most appalling front in order to clear north

Denmark. I was all for staying over another day but I think most of us at one time or another have suffered from that appalling disease of 'get-home-itis'. There is obviously no place like home but coupled with the guilt that you are having a good time and should not have too much of a good time otherwise you will spoil it for the others, there is always this tendency to push for home and on one or two occasions I have to admit we pushed things just that little bit too far. And despite a downfall of the most enormous hailstones we got away with just a few dents at the front of the aircraft.

Monday 4 July saw the start of a deployment of some twelve aircraft of the squadron to the Eifel region of Germany. I was to fly with Norrie Rough and Bob Sutton was our crewman. By this stage I had developed a reasonable level of competence and whenever we went on a major exercise we flew as two pilots with a crewman. Norrie would do some of the more demanding work and I would pick up the loose ends while gaining experience. It was great fast flying round the Eifel. It is a particularly picturesque area; lots of rolling hills and ideal territory to fly a helicopter really down low and enjoy things. One of the things I remember particularly about the exercise was that we had widely dispersed from the flight location and we parked in a fire break between some tall trees. We were listening out on the radio waiting to be called back from our headquarters. Obviously we had not taken things too seriously up to that point and when a group of about eight or nine infantrymen surrounded us about ten or twelve feet away and started firing their machine gun blanks, Norrie Rough stood up and said he had had quite enough, walked down to the head of this group and said, 'Why don't you lot bugger off and play your war games somewhere else?' They stopped firing and turned around and went off. Norrie was quite an intimidating guy when he wanted to be. I do not know what happened in the debrief or whether anyone was told.

I have to say that also there was a lot that the seniors organising these exercises and deployments did not see. On a couple of occasions during our rigorous nights in the field, several us would tie the aircraft down, toss a coin to see who had to stay behind and the rest would go down to the local pub, but be back in time either to check in on the radio or be ready for the early morning launches. In fact one of the sneaky things we would do on these exercises was to telephone the nearest civilian airport and find out whether any warnings had been issued about any military helicopter activity during the night and if they had not then we knew we would not be flying and we would be safe in the pub.

Another thing that happened very regularly on these exercises on the Continent was that the local kids would appear from nowhere. We tried to make it a matter of pride to be able to secrete ourselves in woodland clearings either in the twilight or the very early hours of the day so that no one would see us going in, and yet within a quarter of an hour or so of arriving somewhere, the kids would be there on their bicycles asking for one or two marks to go and fetch the provisions of the day. And they were very good; they would go and fetch a newspaper or some fresh food so that we could cook it on our little Tommy cookers, and it did not matter how much you gave them, they would come back with the correct change and expect you to pay them the agreed amount.

Most of that summer, my first summer on operational squadron, was spent either on exercise or in Northern

Ireland and I spent very little time at home. On Wednesday 27 August it was a particularly rainy and blustery summer afternoon and I was on duty in the crew room at Aldergrove when we were scrambled to fly a search and rescue mission off the coast of Antrim. I flew it with Derek Whatling, 'Fat Man' as he was known. Derek was a search and rescue expert who was doing what he hoped would be a short sojourn with 72 Squadron, the support helicopter squadron. Off we went to drag an Irishman off his boat. The man later told us he was sailing round the world. It seemed that this particular excursion was about fifty minutes old when he ran into trouble. I believe he tried again a few months later and put the search and rescue services to the same amount of trouble.

Between Tuesday 6 and Thursday 8 September, some six months after arriving on my squadron, I flew my C Category upgrade with Tony Jones. Our squadron, as indeed all of the support helicopter squadrons, was a part of 38 Group and the standardisation system among the air crew was to award a Category of A to E. To ensure the highest standards were maintained, a number of the more gifted air crew were detailed to assess our flying standards. This test would take a number of days involving flying sorties by day and night. You normally arrived on the squadron with a D Category and after about a year or so you could attempt to upgrade to C. At this stage in my career I was doing particularly well because after only six months I managed to achieve the upgrade to C.

During an exercise in North Wales in the early part of November 1977 I had cause to make a claim through the accounts system for some toiletries. The officer in charge of accounts went absolutely doo-lally. My claim was only for a few pounds but for some reason I had not filled in the paperwork correctly and while I eventually got my money it took a great deal of effort to do so.

On Monday 7 November I was tasked to fly to Lichfield. I cannot remember particularly what I was doing – I think it was something in support of some Army training – but just as the task was complete and we were making our way back to Odiham I got the message to get the aircraft into cover just as quickly as possible. A freak weather system had developed and it meant that storm force winds were about to lash most of the country. I had about an hour and a half maximum before the weather would hit the aircraft and if it was out in the open it would almost certainly do it some damage. I was flying with my old pal Keith Munday, 'King Rat', and we agreed without hesitation that Birmingham airport would be the best place to go. Not only would they be able to offer us professional assistance and get the aircraft into a hangar but also we would be able to claim allowances for overnight accommodation away from military hospitality. We talked to the controllers at Birmingham on the way in and by the time we reached the airfield the wind was already well over 50mph. Most civilian flights had been diverted elsewhere and I sat with my aircraft in the hover for about forty minutes because the wind was too strong for me to close down. At one stage we carried out a short refuel. They managed to get some light aircraft out of a hangar into the lee of the building where they would be safe and then I taxied inside the hangar and shut down.

With the aircraft safely put to bed in the hangar at Birmingham it was time for Keith and me to look after our own requirements. Neither of us had taken any diversion kit at all. The task had been a day trip out from Odiham to Lichfield and we were expecting to be back by late afternoon. Mindful of the run in I had had with OC accounts at Odiham some days before I decided that this time, rather than make a claim, I would do what we were supposed to do and that was to talk to the local handling agent – which in this case was British Airways – and ask them to organise our overnight stay.

As a captain of a Royal Air Force aircraft I was given a suite of rooms in the Excelsior Hotel, which was the main hotel for the airport at the time. I even had a taxi ride to take me the 200 yards from the terminal building to the hotel and it was insisted that a porter should carry my nav-bag. It was all really way over the top but when British Airways handle you they certainly do it in style. A sumptuous meal in the hotel rounded off a perfect evening and the hotel manager reminded me discreetly that any drinks would probably find themselves included in the cost of either my evening meal or breakfast. All I had to do during the evening, the night and the following morning was sign bits of paper which I duly did. I thought I would enjoy it while I could and bear the consequences when the accounts system next caught up with me.

In fact OC accounts was in touch within a very short time of me getting back, asking me to go to his office to sign some pieces of paper. I went along to his office to find that what had happened was that my signature had not gone through to the final copy so would I please sign the piece of paper. I looked and the bill for mine and Keith's accommodation and looking after the helicopter at Birmingham airport had come to thousands of pounds. OC accounts did not mind in the least that it was so much as long as the paperwork was in order. He could not see my humour and astonishment that having got things wrong some weeks before to the tune of a few pounds –

certainly under a tenner – as long as the paperwork was in order it was okay for me to spend thousands at the taxpayer's expense.

From Monday 21 to Friday 25 November I was involved in a major exercise on Salisbury Plain – Exercise Avon Express. This involved bridge attacks, concealed approaches, night operations – and it was the night operations which began to frighten me quite a lot. We were being called upon to do some pretty challenging stuff at very low level and I was not sure whether we were all up to it or not. In the event, at the end of the exercise there were one or two rather ashen faces and certainly a few huddles as people discussed the particular frights they had endured. But fortunately no one was hurt.

Up until now I had just been enjoying myself, having a whale of a time flying the Wessex and really not taking anything too seriously other than the fact that I wanted to be a good RAF pilot. There was still a tremendous undertow on the morale front. Lots of guys, particularly the experienced ones, were very keen to leave the service, feeling that they had been mushrooms for long enough. Even after being on the squadron for only seven or eight months I still detected that there was this determination to go from an amateur outfit to a professional one. I think those of us on the inside who wanted at the time to make a full career of the service were very keen for those who wanted to go to the oil rigs to bugger off and leave us to it.

Around the middle of December a couple of us and two helicopters were deployed to Valley to do some mountain flying in Snowdonia and this really was great stuff. I teamed up with Pete Beglan. He was a very experienced search and rescue pilot who was spending a tour on

72 Squadron prior, he hoped, to going back to search and rescue. He was very experienced particularly in the skills of mountain flying. Pete had his own dog, a little wire-haired terrier called Tuppence who used to sit on the dashboard whenever he flew. The mountain flying itself went reasonably well and without hassle. We had a good few nights in the mess at Valley, taking the mickey out of the fighter pilot trainees and me secretly wishing that I was back there with them having failed just a couple of years previously.

On the way back from Valley to Odiham we planned to refuel at Stafford, and we were about two or three miles away from Stafford on the approach when we suffered a starboard engine fire warning. Fire in a helicopter is the most terrifying of scenarios, particularly if you are flying along at anything other than a fairly low level, because the chances are that the aircraft will be burned to a cinder before it reaches the ground. We quickly managed to slam it onto the ground at Stafford and shut down having discharged the extinguishers into the engine. When we had a look we could not find anything much wrong with it. It may have been just a spurious warning, but you never take too many chances with this stuff.

As it was, it was Friday 16 December and Pete made a very daring decision that we should leave the aircraft there and catch the train back to Odiham in time to be in the bar for at least the last hour or so before it closed. We got on the train – myself, Pete and Airdog Tuppence – tickets courtesy of the guard room, Stafford. But we only managed to stay at Odiham for an hour or so when Flight Commander Jim Clarkson ranted and raved to the effect that the one thing you never do is leave your aircraft anywhere, you go back and fetch it. And so at first light another aircraft with spares and an engineer to fix things went back up to Stafford. The repair was fairly straightforward and so I flew it home on Saturday.

On the evening of Thursday 5 January 1978, after a Christmas at home, I was back in Northern Ireland. There was a fairly heated conversation going on in the Scruffs Bar between myself, a few other hardened drinkers and Flight Commander Jim Clarkson. I felt that I was long overdue for my combat-ready check and a pilot in the Air Force never keeps his wings until he has passed a combat-ready check. This normally takes place within the first year of service on the squadron and it implies that you have gone through most of the training now and you are safe to hone your skills as a fully combat-ready RAF pilot. Clarkson agreed that I was ready and that as soon as a decent opportunity arose I would fly my combat-ready check with him, my flight commander, as was the tradition. The conversation went on to other mundane things but it certainly lasted well until sunrise – a good thing I had got nothing planned for the Friday which was to be a free day.

I could not have been in bed for more than an hour when all hell let loose. It seemed that there had been some terrorist activity in the province and I still do not recall to this day precisely what it was, but basically I was bundled onto the spare wheel of a Land Rover, which is on the bonnet of the vehicle, doused with a bucket of water and driven up and down the main road outside the support helicopter headquarters in an effort to get me sober. Jim Clarkson was one of those infuriating men who could drink for fourteen hours, sleep for thirty-five minutes and be ready for another full day's drinking.

'Now is your chance Mason,' he screamed with glee.

113

'It's your combat-ready check – the perfect opportunity.' I felt like death and stumbled up the side of the helicopter. Before I managed to start one of the engines I felt incredibly sick and Squadron Leader Clarkson could see from my desperate pallor I was going to be no use to man nor beast. However, we persevered for the moment. I managed to get the helicopter airborne and we stumbled off to the north towards Antrim but by this stage I was feeling much the worse for wear and certainly should not have been anywhere near an aircraft; a pair of roller skates would have been way beyond my capability for that matter.

We landed in a woodland clearing and shut the aircraft down – something decidedly against the rules, very risky. Brian Mills, who was the crewman, helped me from the aircraft and put me down into the cabin. That is about all I remember until later that evening, something like about nine or ten hours later, I woke up freezing cold in the back of the Wessex which was closed down in the hangar at Aldergrove. Jim Clarkson and Brian Mills had flown the trip entirely on their own with me in the rear pylon fast asleep.

I managed to find my way out of the hangar having woken up the duty policeman by setting off one of the alarms. He was well primed that at some stage I would be finding my way out and gave me a lift down to the officers' mess. I went into the Scruffs Bar and there sure enough was Jim Clarkson leading the singing. 'Your round Mason,' he screamed from afar as I entered. It seemed that I had to buy the beers – I had flown my combat ready check and passed it. And still to this day I have no idea what I did.

It was in January shortly after getting back from

Northern Ireland that I bought my boat. It was a cabin cruiser that I kept on the Thames for the next couple of years. I shared it with Euan Alexander, a close friend of mine who was on 33 Squadron flying Pumas. For each of us it was like having our own boat – we spent so much time away on detachment that because we were on different squadrons we tended to be away at different times. By good organisation we agreed precisely how much we could afford for our boat and we spent two or three days searching all of the boatyards on the Thames. When we did buy the boat we spent exactly three times the amount we believed we could possibly afford. It just goes to show that you can always afford what you really want.

It was also around this time that Squadron Leader Clarkson ordered me to get my General Service Medal and have it sewn onto my uniform. Some weeks prior to that I had been to a full parade at RAF Cranwell where a colleague of mine had been presented with his General Service Medal. The medal was awarded to anyone who had spent more than a month in a theatre of action and Northern Ireland was deemed to be a place where you risked getting your head shot off. As I had spent well over a month there it was time to get my medal, it just did not seem terribly important. But I trotted off to the clothing stores and there at Supply Squadron the corporal said that he had my medal ready for me. He got my name and rank and stencilled round the outside, and the green and purple ribbon was attached to it so that I could sew a ribbon or get a ribbon sewn onto my uniform. I asked him if there was some form of presentation in awarding the medal and the corporal stood smartly to attention and said, 'I hereby present you with your General Service Medal, Sir. Sign here.'

At the end of January 1978 came a week of the most exciting flying that I have ever had. It was Sunday 29 January approaching lunchtime and I was working in a very cold and draughty garage repairing the cylinder head to a rather aged Ford Cortina. Up until now I had had very nice cars but having bought the boat I sold the car in order to raise my half of the cash and was now driving around in a really very battered red and black Cortina. The previous week I had been a Duty Pilot on the Sunday and the aircraft had been called to a scramble. Every RAF flying mission has to be authorised by a senior crew member who is also qualified to authorise his own flying. The authoriser had been Squadron Leader Clarkson and he decided that he was going to fly the trip and I could sit down and watch the desk. I had complained bitterly about this, saying that he should have authorised it and I should have flown it.

So here I was in the garage on 29 January, the telephone rang and I needed to get into work quickly with a bag packed for at least two or three days away. I had been listening to the news on the car radio. It had been snowing and blizzarding in Scotland for about forty-eight hours now. Many roads had been cut off, a train had been lost in the northern Highlands and the place was getting in quite a desperate state. When the phone rang and I was called to pack my bag I put the two together and made four. It was a scramble to provide search and rescue cover in Scotland.

Flight Sergeant Rick Shepherd was the crewman and within an hour we were airborne from Odiham and, refuelling en route first at Waddington and then Leeming, we reached Leuchars that evening. By first light the following morning we were at work. I could almost write a book on what happened that week. I flew for almost thirty hours in seven days. Thirty hours would be a respectable target for a month's flying. On one approach to an isolated farm I flew through some wires that had already been brought down by the storm and was whipped up by my down wash. The wires tore two or three holes in the rotor blades making the aircraft almost totally uncontrollable, but we managed to limp to the High Range Motel in Aviemore where I shut down on a central reservation. A couple of hours later I was asked by a local to move it so he could get his car out and the answer was an emphatic 'No'. The helicopter was repaired the following morning with a civilian team from Bristows flown in to fix it and we were back at work at first light.

I remember landing at one rather palatial home to make sure that the family was okay. The gentleman looked at me very sheepishly asking me if my aircraft was all right. I assured him that it was and asked him what his concern was. This concern was that I had landed right on top of his swimming pool.

Each night we stayed in a lovely hotel somewhere along the route but only after a full twelve or thirteen hours work. A local gamekeeper gave me the most marvellous otter skin. It was also the time when I had my first encounters with the press and TV. I have to say that in many ways they were not pleasant ones. I was persuaded to fly a reporter, when we had just a little bit of spare space, as we went to pick up some people from an isolated hamlet or something. I asked for his complete discretion, saying that he could come along and just have a look at what was going on without actually mentioning anyone by name. The next time I saw myself I was staring from the front page of the *Scottish Daily Mirror* and underneath in large type

'Little Short of Heroic'. People queued up to have their photographs taken with me.

I have to say that the RAF organisation for this search and rescue mission in Scotland in early 1978 was absolutely superb, it was almost faultless. We had a Shackleton flying overhead twenty-four hours a day and he would book everything for us from fuel to hotel accommodation. As soon as we were feeling slightly short of fuel he would organise a rendezvous and a Bristows helicopter would arrive with a couple of drums of fuel for us to take on board.

I felt part of this amazing team and I certainly feel that we did a great deal for the people of Scotland. We learned a lot as well. You take batteries to outlying areas and not food. The people are well prepared with food for these long stays but what they had not got was batteries and transistor radios. Needless to say, they had lost their electricity supply in the early hours of the week. People were fantastic, they all pulled together and everybody seemed to think that there must be lots of others in a far worse situation than they were. It was like the Blitz spirit.

About three or four days into the operation we came across a tramp. He had been frozen to the road. Obviously at an early stage he had just fallen asleep at the roadside, then when he had woken up he could not lift himself. A couple of nights in hospital and he was right as rain, back on the road again. We found a couple in an upturned car. They were in their late fifties and it really did take a tremendous amount of effort from myself and Rick to get them to leave their car. There they were quite happy, they had their flask and some warm drinks left – if we could give them some hot water they would be fine; shouldn't we go and look for some people who were in a worse state than them? Eventually we coaxed them into the helicopter and flew them into Aviemore where they were greeted by the press and the medical services.

At one particular place the people had given me half a bottle of fine Scotch whisky. When we landed at the end of the day Rick climbed onto an OLEO (the main undercarriage leg) and passed me the bottle just as the aircraft shut down. A couple of amused policeman watched as I removed the top and took a fairly healthy swig just to keep the cold out. Rick told them it was okay, I was down to two bottles a day now.

We came across a bungalow on the junction on the A9 and landed to see if we could provide any help to the people there. It was a small two-bedroomed retirement bungalow and between us, that is ourselves and another two Wessex helicopters, we airlifted thirty people out of it.

By 5 February, seven days later, it was all over and with the half dozen or so helicopters that had flown up to join us, we flew back into Odiham to a hero's welcome. It was just amazing, the warm and comfortable feeling to have played a part in that sort of operation. I think up until then I had maybe felt just a little bit of resentment that I had not got to be a fighter pilot and I felt maybe even second rate, but that week in Scotland, doing the job for which I had been trained and doing it very well indeed, I just felt so proud of myself that I did not want any recognition from anyone else. I felt this tremendous sense of achievement.

It was at an exercise on Salisbury Plain on 23 and 24 February, Exercise Flying Fox, that I think I started comparing the ways of life of an Army officer and a Royal

Air Force officer. One of the simple ways to describe it is how it was explained to me, and that is when you take the three services as they go to war they do it in entirely different ways. In the Navy the officers and the men go to war together; they are all strapped down in their ship. In the Air Force the men send the officers off to war, and in the Army the officers send the men.

Monday 6 March 1978 I was on an exercise MINEVAL. We were scrambled to rescue a crashed helicopter and I was flying with Jon Hockin. Jon was a very pleasant chap who had spent some time with the Army Air Corps and had his own way of doing a number of things. He was studying hard to become a company accountant when he left the Air Force a year or so later. The crashed helicopter we were sent to rescue was in fact the old fire training wreck that had been towed out on the back of a lorry and had been put in a field. Unfortunately Jon decided to approach too close to the wreck and in the final stages of the approach we blew just about everything away.

On Monday 24 April I almost got away with it. I had been tasked with a day mission from Odiham to Aldergrove to pick up another helicopter and bring it straight back to Odiham. I was actually in the operations room at Aldergrove and I was just about to leave for home when someone offered me a little job which I simply could not refuse. Please could I take this lovely old cart and drop it off at his father's house at Ruthin in Wales. Oh and by the way there was a donkey to go with the cart! It seemed like a good idea to me and so fairly discreetly we loaded the animal and the cart into the helicopter and set off.

I managed to get to Ruthin at last light and at the appointed grid reference there was a gentleman waiting for me who was the father of the Army major who owned the said donkey and cart. He thanked me profusely, saying he did not know how they would have got the animal and vehicle back without my help and I just asked if he could stay as discreet as possible as I was fairly sure the higher-ups would not understand what I had done. A couple of weeks later a fuming Wing Commander Salter demanded my presence in his office. There was a case of whisky, a thank-you letter and a photograph of the donkey and cart in situ on the farm. I do not think the wing commander was too annoyed. We shared the whisky out among the squadron at the next squadron bash.

On 27 June 1978, a Tuesday afternoon, I was flying the normal task at Brize Norton when we were ordered to divert to the Royal Naval Air Station at Culdrose on a compassionate 'A'. Compassionate 'A' is normally a situation where someone is very close to death and they need to get their close family to them as quickly as possible, which is where the military is brought into play. I do not know the full circumstances but I picked up a lady at Brize Norton and flew her across to Culdrose. There was a Royal Flight helicopter at Culdrose which we followed in to land. I think that she got on that helicopter and went from there onwards but I still do not know where.

During the summer of 1978 there were one or two marvellous incidents with a Pack Howitzer. This is a massive field gun which could just about be lifted by a Wessex. A Puma, with its slightly higher payload, could lift it a deal easier. The Operational Conversion Unit at Odiham was given an old Pack Howitzer to practise under-slung load work. When not in use this was left at the side of the hangar. Fortunately it was all too easy to get hold of. Brian Freeman, who I think is now a wing commander or a group captain, was duly enrolled along with his Renault car. We towed this cannon about the place. On one occasion a group of us fired a tin of fruit juice straight through the wall and roof of the hangar of the Operational Conversion Unit and on another occasion the gun was fired again sending a couple of tins of fruit juice straight through the front doors of the officers' mess. The total bill to six of us came to almost £2,000 so I had to enlist the help of my dad at very short notice to help repair the doors.

Tuesday 8 to Friday 11 August 1978 saw me involved in some pre-Northern Ireland training for the Scots Guards. In one of the several training areas in the United Kingdom we aimed to make life as realistic as possible to prepare them for the operations they were about to face in Northern Ireland. However, the senior officers asked us if we could drop them off in London at Chelsea Barracks to stop for tea – and it really was a case of how the other half lives.

Another incident in Northern Ireland happened on Saturday 26 August 1978. I had been a smoker for a number of years, although on various occasions and in numerous ways I had tried either to give it up or cut down. This was a phase when I was smoking a pipe and my lovely Meerschaum pipe had fallen to the floor and shattered. For several days I had been making most people's lives hell. It was decided enough was enough and I was dispatched with Flight Lieutenant Barrie Simmonds, known as Simmo, and Sergeant Arter to Machrihanish in Scotland. (I saw Arter recently; he now works for Midland Air Services at Birmingham airport.) The dispatch as far as I was concerned was simply a dry run to Scotland but as soon as we had landed at Machrihanish there was a police car to meet us. We landed the aircraft on the town square and

Air Cadet Summer Camp at
RAF Leuchars in 1965 with
me in the centre, standing.

ust before joining the RAF
n September 1973, with
ny pride and joy - a home-
uilt 650cc motor bike.

The first official photograph of Officer
Cadet P J D Mason.

Left 'Pleased as Punch' - a safe landing from my first solo flight in a jet aircraft, 14 March 1974.

Below Early days in close formation over the Vale of the White Horse in Yorkshire. The aircraft is a Jet Provost T Mk5.

Left
A few weeks before receiving my 'Wings', December 1974.

Right
Pilot Officer Mason is awarded his RAF Wings, 10 January 1975. One of the proudest moments of my life.

Some of the successful graduates from the advanced jet course at RAF Valley in North Wales, September 1975. Only five made it through to fighters at the first attempt. The aircraft is a Folland Gnat T Mk1.

Preparing to lift an underslung load in a Wessex HC Mk2 over Northern Ireland, January 1977.

Top left 1,000 flying hours on the Wessex HC Mk2, shared with Sid Exton, 19 September 1979. Squadron Leader Martin Gardiner pours the champagne.

Top right Yet another morning after the night before in Northern Ireland. Jim Clarkson, Hugh Northey, me and Paul O'Brennan.

Middle left A safe landing on the A9 at Aviemore, having just flown through some power cables, during the winter operations of early 1978.

Bottom left An impromptu fly-past in Hong Kong on New Year's Eve 1980 The photograph was taken from my living-room window

The aircrew of 28 Squadron, January 1981. As usual, I am at the centre of things!

A squadron photograph with a difference.
Taken during the summer of 1981. The aircraft is a 1930s Tiger Moth
trainer which I borrowed from my pal David Baker.

Above Taken over Barnstaple Bay just before Pete Sheppard and I ejected, 29 July 1983. Look again. The entire front section is missing from the Hawk T Mk1.

Left Eleanor, Daddy and Michael, August 1983.

Below Les Pearce and yours truly after a very heavy weekend in southern Italy, summer 1985.

One thousand flying hours on the Tornado GR Mk1, celebrated with friends from 16 Squadron at RAF Laarbruch, 20 June 1988.

The team at Decimomannu in Sardinia. Centre stage again!

Left A wet arrival on XV Squadron, August 1988.

Below A XV Squadron Tornado in its 75th Anniversary livery over the Mohne Dam (made famous by the Dambuster raids), summer 1990.

Above In our pet shop with Saddam Hussein, a young Scarlet Macaw.

Below On the flight deck of an Airtours Boeing 757 with my son Michael.

the police car drove us up to the local tobacconist where I bought myself a new pipe and was given a complimentary few ounces of tobacco. Then we flew back to Aldergrove. The pipe itself cost £5.03 but as the trip to and from Machrihanish had taken an hour it was known as the £2,005.03 pipe – a Wessex in those days costing around £2,000 an hour to operate.

From Monday 11 September until Tuesday 26 September 1978 I took part in a CSRO course (combat, survival and rescue officers course) at RAF Mountbatten near Plymouth. Once again the course itself was something you could write a book about as many people indeed have. The Royal Air Force survival courses are renowned throughout the world as among the most educational and certainly the most arduous.

Basically the first week you spend in the classroom learning how to survive in various environments but principally, of course, considering the European theatre. It was ten days of absolute hell. You then get a chance to put into practice all of those hours spent in the classroom. For us the location was Dartmoor. You spend the first couple of days on your own. I think I was allowed a parachute and five cigarettes. You have to cover a number of miles each day and meet for further instructions at grid references. But you also spend several phases being searched for by, in our case, members of the local marines commando.

After a couple of days you are teamed up with another member of the course and then after another couple of days you all get together in one area. It is how most people would imagine, only worse. You make shelters from bits of parachute and whatever else you can forage. You learn how to hide, you learn to move as stealthily as you can.

The amusing interlude during this was when Taff Morgan, who was the guy I teamed up with, and I had spent hours and hours making a fishing net from the nylon strands of parachute cable. We left the net half made between two trees and during the night – a fitful, cold, damp sleep – there was the most incredible screaming noise. At the time we both denied completely hearing it but the following morning when we went out to our fishing net there caught in it was a dead cormorant and it was that that had been making the screaming noise. At this stage we had not eaten anything substantial for about a week and the cormorant was soon consigned to the pot and we shared it with a couple of other guys. It tastes like salty steak.

We learned how to tickle trout and on 20 September, which was my twenty-eighth birthday, I went to sort out my traps and in one of them I found a bottle of tomato sauce – the instructors were human after all. The instructor was a man called Geordie Scott and he was known worldwide for his expertise in teaching people how to survive. He had a lot to do with teaching the Special Air Service Regiment.

I made friends for life during that course. I have already mentioned Taff Morgan who I was teamed up with during the final stages of the actual survival course itself. Bill Purchase was a squadron leader Canberra pilot who I bumped into several times during my Air Force career. We always shared a fond memory and recollection of what had gone on during those weeks in September. Students came to the course from all over the world – I stayed friends with Anker Sorrensen who was a Norwegian, a very good survivor and a demon skier. Then there was François – I cannot remember his surname – a French Air Force officer.

I learned how to kill animals for food and after a few days we were given a live chicken each which was dispatched quite easily. It is amazing what you will do when you are really hungry. At the end of the course you go through an interrogation and it is something I would not like to go through again. My interrogation lasted about twenty-four hours – at the time it felt like weeks and weeks. It was done very, very realistically. The interrogators wore Russian uniforms and if there were more than one of them in the room at any one time they always talked to each other in Russian. Fortunately from my school days I had a smattering of Russian so I could recognise the language.

Our training had been to give away nothing other than name, rank, serial number and date of birth and the only other comment was 'I cannot answer that question, Sir'. A number of men in the Royal Air Force have been broken as a result of just training for interrogation. At the end of it all I enjoyed the biggest breakfast in the world – three of everything and off to bed. I slept for about fifteen or sixteen hours I think. I never enjoyed a shave so much in my life.

From Tuesday 3 October until Sunday 15 October I was on exercise in Germany. Our crewman was Sergeant Bob Cuthill. He was a broad Brummie and had the envied reputation of always being able to provide hot tea whenever and wherever it was required. The main thing that sticks in my mind was the explosive night of Saturday 14 October at Wildenrath. It was a night that almost went down in history and could have been a damn sight more fatal than it was. Over the two weeks of the exercise Simmo and myself had accumulated quite a lot of explosive. It started off with just having thunder flashes, which are peacetime exercise grenades. But things had just blossomed and through various barterings and swaps we ended up with quite a lot of plastic explosive complete with electric detonators.

The night got very boozy very early and there was also a lot of frustration. We had had two weeks in the field and when Wildenrath offered us their hospitality we decided to take it up. However, what we were offered and what we received were two different things. We were accommodated in the transit blocks which quite frankly were appalling. There were not even any mattresses on the beds. No one had any keys to the door so we had to get in through a window, the place was draughty and very, very dreary.

Simmo and I decided that we'd had enough and that it was time to liven things up. Shortly after the bar closed, we went back to the helicopter, picked up some explosive and started to blow things up. It started off with a couple of trees in a forest clearing fairly close to the operations centre. We then made a big bang fairly near to the operation centre itself, and finally, approaching our coup de grâce, we set some plastic explosive around a door at the end of the accommodation block. The idea was that we would blow the door open so we could get inside and find somewhere to sleep. But unfortunately with this resounding explosion still ringing in our ears we looked up to see that while the door was still standing, albeit only for a few seconds longer, the entire end of the building had been blown out and the roof had collapsed. Most of the thirty or forty inmates inside, all of whom were our fellow support helicopter operators, had stayed fast asleep as they too had enjoyed a fairly boozy evening – only one or two woke up to wonder what that noise was. Some of them slept with the ceiling of the building only two or three inches from their noses. No one had a scratch. We led charmed lives.

The following morning Simmo and I were marched up in front of the station commander at Wildenrath and it is fair to say that he was absolutely fuming. He wanted us court martialled and then shot, whether we were found guilty or not I think. Anyway we were able to get away with it really quite well because we had proved to be quite an embarrassment to the Quick Reaction Forces at Wildenrath. Unbeknown to us, three or four hours before I was caught fast asleep on the lawn outside the transit block, the Quick Reaction Force had been issued with live ammunition. It was felt that a terrorist attack was in progress, while all that was happening was two very drunk support helicopter pilots were wreaking havoc with some explosive they had left over from the exercise.

To have made the matter public in the form of a court martial, which it certainly warranted, would have been a severe embarrassment to the station commander and his team and so it was we just had a horrendous bollocking each accompanied by a horrendous headache. Simmo was transported to Northern Ireland where he served for three months on the ground and I got a number of nasty little jobs for a while. In fact I was banned from exercises in Germany for twelve months. But they could not keep the ban up as they were running out of pilots.

On Thursday 16 February 1979, a particularly cold and frosty morning, I was tasked to go to Sywell, which is a small civilian airfield not very far from Peterborough, with a spare engine for Gary Thomas's Wessex. His aircraft had taken in some ice during a snow storm and the engine was a write off and needed replacing. I got to

Gary in good time and then carried on to Wittering to refuel prior to returning to Odiham. The engineer was fixing Gary's helicopter and he would be flying it back just as soon as the new engine was in situ. It was while waiting for my refuel at Wittering that the squadron leader in charge of operations there asked if I could help with a casualty evacuation of a pregnant woman to hospital. It transpired that the woman was married to one of the Harrier pilots and they lived in a local farm and had been cut off by the appalling weather. By now it was getting fairly dark, the snow was falling and we were in for a not very pleasant night. However, we elected to go because it seemed a pretty urgent situation. We told the people at the farm to put out whatever bright sheets that they could find and secure them to the ground. We got there in reasonable time. By now it was almost dark but we could pick out the farm because of the bright sheets they had put down. We landed, took the woman on board and sure enough she was in the final stages of labour. As we took off and turned towards Peterborough it was now snowing very hard indeed and almost night. I was getting lower and lower. Gary was in the left-hand seat giving me what navigational assistance he could.

We landed in fields a couple of times when it got so bad that you could not see much more than a hand in front of your face. All this time we had been talking to the radar controller at Wittering who was trying to give us whatever assistance he could. It seemed that we were not going to be able to get through to the hospital and now there was myself, Gary and the crewman and a pregnant woman on board and nowhere to go. The controller asked us if we knew where we were, which we did not at the time, but by hover taxiing along the road we picked out a pub.

He then knew precisely where we were and he controlled us along the road telling us where the pylons were and the railway lines were and took us into Peterborough town by describing the roads along which we had to fly. Eventually we came into some playing fields which were just outside the nurses' home and shut down. The helicopter was almost completely covered in ice and was going nowhere that day. Mum gave birth to a baby boy about an hour and a half after we had arrived there. I won't say too much about what happened then but this was 16 February and we did not actually get home until four days later having had to spend several days in the only accommodation available which was the nurses' home of the Peterborough General Hospital. It was with great pride that we learned subsequently that the child had been called Paul Gareth in honour of the two pilots who had flown Mum to hospital.

I had been involved in some pretty heavy high jinks up until now, mostly revolving around the bar and Friday night happenings. I was almost caught this time teaching Bunty, my Old English sheepdog, to drive. I am not sure what possessed me to do it but it seemed like a good idea at the time. On the night of Friday 9 March 1979 I had been involved in an exercise in Germany, Exercise Joyful Caper, and we were out in Hammelin having a good few beers. I think that one of the things that you used to find out in Germany as soon as they knew you were Royal Air Force, was how locals would be quick to boast of their own tales of derring-do either on the Russian front or flying the Spitfire's formidable adversary, the Messerschmitt ME-109. At this particular bar I met this particular guy who seemed to have done both. We took an instant dislike to each other and had a bit of a fight. I left the bar, much the worse for wear, with the bar stool under my arm, was subsequently arrested by the military police and spent a night in the cells.

Before the next week on this exercise I did not do any flying at all – I was involved in the running of the operations, or helping to run the operations while the squadron commander decided what to do with me. It seemed as though I was going to get some form of disciplinary action. The best thing for me to do, if I could, was get out of there until the dust had settled. And so, having got back from exercise on 17 March I managed to organise myself onto the Officers' Command School at Royal Air Force Henlow, which was a month's course in office management and general communication and organisation skills. Our syndicate commander was a guy called Squadron Leader Alan Middleton.

It was good news that I met up with him because at the end of the third week of the school I was recalled to 72 Squadron to be given a formal warning by my Squadron Commander, Wing Commander Ryles. I took Squadron Leader Middleton with me asking if he would help me out of this jam as far as he could. Initially the wing commander wanted to court martial me but Squadron Leader Middleton persuaded him that perhaps there was some hope, and so it was watered down to a formal warning which meant that I was going to spend more time as a Flying Officer before I could be promoted to Flight Lieutenant and of course be watched rather closely. It was about this time in my annual confidential report that the station commander wrote that he had never met a junior officer who did so much to further his own career while at the same time doing almost as much to destroy it.

There was the occasion during an exercise in mid-July of 1979 where we were training some Officer Cadets at the

Stamford Practical Training Area at Watton. RAF Watton had almost run down to nothing but the officers' mess was still in existence and provided a facility for Eastern Radar. An amusing little incident was when we arrived outside the officers' mess in our Wessex helicopters and put them inside the tennis court so that they would be securely surrounded by a wire fence for the evening. The embarrassment was that no one had a key to the tennis court and so we were in there and could not get out. The only solutions were either to climb over the fence or start the helicopters up again and land them outside the courts which is what we did.

In August of 1979 I, Al Rogers and Laurie Playle went sailing on Al Rogers' tiny little boat called *'Alor Star'*. We sailed for a weekend around the Isle of Wight during a force eight gale when no one else would go out. We did not realise that the coast guards had been called out for us and a Royal Navy helicopter came out looking for us. They thought no one but idiots would be sailing in that. It was the first time I had ever been sailing at sea and I thought it was always like that. It was great fun although we made a bit of a mess of Al's sails when they were ripped to shreds during the storm force winds.

In September of 1979 I was involved in the Mountbatten incident in Northern Ireland and was also, of course, at Warrenpoint when twenty odd Guards were blown up. Mountbatten's life was taken from him without him even knowing that he was in a battle.

From Monday 22 October to Thursday 25 October I went on a Germany trainer with Wing Commander Ryles and Duncan McDougal, a very well-respected crewman who was about six feet four inches tall and had the most incredibly large hands. He was known as the biggest crewman in the world. It was felt that with the wing commander and Duncan McDougal looking after me I could not get into any more trouble. On the Wednesday afternoon I went off with just Duncan and did a training trip. Fortunately we managed to keep it from the wing commander that there had been some complaints about a Wessex flying low-level bombing-type runs against the Mohne Dam, flying the replica path to that of the Dambusters' raid. It just seemed too good to resist.

There was an incident towards the end of 1979 when I was ordered to go out to Salisbury Plain to lay out a night tee. Basically this consists five bright white lights laid out in the shape of a 'T' which is surveyed during the day so that helicopters can approach them at night. I laid the tee out along with its associated aids and switched everything on. There was an hour or so to spare until the first helicopters arrived so I went down with my two airmen assistants to the local pub to get a beer in before the helicopters came. I was supposed to be at the tee to wait for the helicopters and to monitor them around the circuit. Well, needless to say we got chatting and playing pool when we heard this Wessex come in low over the pub and calling in on the radio. The only thing I could do was get the radio into the pub and start talking to them as though I was out there in the field. This I did and all worked well for an hour or so until the last helicopter, containing my flight commander, offered me a lift home rather than me having to go in the Land Rover. First of all I declined but he insisted. There was nothing for it but to make a run for it so we threw the radio into the Land Rover, rushed off towards the tee which was about a quarter of an hour's drive away across the field with me still talking to him and giving him all the delaying tactics I could by asking him to fly the circuit again. When I eventually got on board the helicopter, completely out of breath, my flight commander looked down at me with a very wry smile and said, 'I don't suppose you'll do that again will you?' He knew exactly where I had been hiding.

On Tuesday 26 February 1980, a fairly fresh day, I was hovering overhead RAF Odiham at 10,000 feet dispatching troops six to eight at a time for a free fall before they parachuted to the intersection of the airfield's runways. Three days later at 9.18p.m. I could have been at 10,000 feet without a helicopter or anything because my son Michael was born. I was still getting over the shock and the self-congratulation and I had phoned the various parents when about 10 o'clock there was a very matter-of-fact call for me. The matron ushered me to a telephone. It was my Flight Commander, Martin Gardener, 'Come on then, what is it?' I told him I was the proud father of a bouncy baby boy. His reply was, 'Get your arse in gear and straight back here because we are keeping the pub open for you.'

It was a Friday night and it was one of the first happy hours that I had ever missed since being at Odiham. I was back shortly before midnight and celebrations went on well into the early hours. The next week was quite a blur but the flight commander had organised a rota of my fellow officers to make sure that each visiting time I was taken along to the hospital, deposited for the regulation time, recovered and brought back home to the pub.

On Saturday 5 April 1980 I managed to wangle a training trip from Aldergrove, which was where I was at the time, across to Stourport on Severn with another pilot and crewman and six or seven of the ground crew for a spot of R & R (rest and relaxation). But it was my excuse to get across to Stourport for my sister Angie's wedding. The wedding was a lovely occasion and by the late afternoon, when it was time for me to return to Ireland, I got on board and was flown back by my fellow pilot John Kennedy and we did a fly past over the reception which Angela still recalls to this day.

Another incident I recall involved a friend of mine. I will call him Len Baker, which is not his real name but I think he would be embarrassed if I were to mention his name. He landed his Puma in his girlfriend's garden on the way back from an exercise. There was a complaint from the neighbour and he got into trouble with the newspapers. What happened was the neighbour was so infuriated that he told Len he was going to write to the station commander to complain. Len, being an officer of renowned initiative, went into the station commander's office first thing every morning for the next week or so and riffled through his mail until he found this letter of complaint. He then wrote a reply in his own words saying that the particular pilot concerned had been severely admonished, that his career would undoubtedly suffer and his promotion delayed by several months. He hoped that the gentleman would accept this as sufficient punishment and consider the matter closed, and then he went away feeling very smug and confident thinking he would hear no more. What he had not planned for was this gentleman being so upset at having destroyed a junior officer's career that not only did he write to the station commander asking that a lesser punishment be meted out but he also wrote to his MP. Len Baker, name changed to protect the guilty, was given a severe bollocking after that.

My conclusions about 72 Squadron, the first three years of my operational Air Force career, are that I left older and wiser. I still wanted fun and I still wanted to enjoy myself. Promotion had been delayed considerably as a result of the formal warning that I had had but I did not regret a single moment of it, any of it.

So now it was a disembarkation leave for a couple of weeks and then my posting to my next tour which was 28 Squadron in Hong Kong.

5

72 Squadron, Northern Ireland

We used to fly out to RAF Aldergrove in Northern Ireland on a Thursday for detachments of six weeks at a time. A Hercules would pop over from Brize Norton for the weekly Northern Ireland changeover – known as NICO. It would arrive on the pan at Odiham to transport about half of the air crew required to maintain the detachment of Pumas and Wessex in the province.

When I was there, there were two Pumas and six Wessex based at Aldergrove. Of the Wessex, any four were on flying duty while the other two underwent maintenance. The three crew of the Wessex were tasked on patrol of border country or transporting soldiers around the countryside while the Puma with its three to four crew was involved in more technical surveillance work. The kit on board the Puma was so sophisticated it was capable of finding something the size of a matchbox buried under the ground.

Half of these crews would change over from Odiham to Aldergrove every three weeks. It was a leap-frog system so that you all completed a six-week stint. But at times there were people who were required to stay on in the province for nine or even twelve weeks.

It was an unaccompanied tour and Sheila, my wife,

remained at Odiham in our married quarter. On one particularly long detachment I was away from home for about three months; from Ireland straight on to exercise in Denmark and then down to Germany. I was expecting to come home for a few days off but ended up being pushed on to Northern Ireland for another six weeks. Squadron Commander Tony Salter met me on the pan at Odiham to tell me I could have the next six hours off to go home and visit my wife. My reply was 'no way' and I promptly climbed aboard the waiting Hercules.

I was not the only flyer who was roped in to that three-month operation. When our turn came finally to fly home to our waiting wives at Odiham we were told that a Hercules that had been sent over to Aldergrove with essential spares could take us home on the Wednesday, twenty-four hours earlier than we had expected. We all sent telegrams to our wives telling them to meet us or that we would be home early. One bright spark – I won't name him because I know his wife would be acutely embarrassed – sent a telegram home instructing her to be waiting on the pan with a mattress strapped to her back. Within hours a telegram arrived for him at Aldergrove. It was from his wife who had replied to warn him 'Husband. You had better be the first one off that Hercules.' That telegram remained pinned to the ops room notice board at Aldergrove.

The rules that existed for air crew on detachment in the province effectively confined us to camp at RAF Aldergrove. We weren't allowed out between the hours of midnight and 8 o'clock in the morning under any circumstances. We couldn't travel in numbers of fewer than two or more than four. And anyone accompanying us had to be a serviceman or woman or a member of their family. On one occasion an officer was caught in flagrante delicto with a young lady he had met on the previous evening in the mess. He was destined to have the book thrown at him until the powers that be were discreetly informed that he hadn't broken any rules. The female concerned in this particular liaison was a military policeman's wife . . .

Needless to say the rules laid down to ensure our safety were broken by us at every and any opportunity. About six of us bought an old Austin Allegro between us for the princely sum of £30. There was no MOT and a close inspection of the tax disc would have revealed a startling similarity to the label from a beer bottle. And anyway, insurance was for wimps. It was a typical family saloon that could comfortably convey four occupants. I've known occasions when there were four occupants in the boot alone and total car capacity close to a dozen.

The military police hated us because there wasn't a lot they could do about our blatant disregard for the rules. Whenever we were pulled over to the side of the road by the MPs they realised that it was far less hassle to send us on our way with the merest of reprimands rather than try to explain to the commander in chief that there would be no support helicopters for the next few days because all of his pilots were in police custody.

One of the easiest ways to escape the confines of our barracks after nightfall was simply to hop aboard one of the regularly patrolling helicopters, only to be dropped off discreetly at a road corner – and, as we got more blasé, in a local pub car park. The notorious no-go areas for the British armed forces in Northern Ireland included the Falls Road, the Divis Flats in west Belfast and the more rural towns of South Armagh like Newry,

Warrenpoint and Armagh City itself. We drank in pubs in all of these places, rubbing shoulders with Republicans and Protestants alike. It was possible to walk into an IRA or Protestant pub without serious risk of attack, though of course we were careful not to visit the same place at the same time in a regular basis. It was all an adventure and we didn't give a toss. Those like myself who could adopt a convincing Irish accent did the talking while everyone did the drinking.

After one night of serious drinking with a pub full of provos, one local began to ask a few awkward questions about where I was from. I continued blathering in my adopted Northern Ireland accent until another drinker threw his arm around me and declared to the rest of the pub: 'to be sure, he is as Irish as the steps of Dublin.'

Far from everyone actually crossed the wires. Only a few of us seriously broke the rules to sample Northern Ireland as it really was. The rest stayed back at our camp drinking in the officers' mess or writing letters home. One fellow pilot, who hardly ever even visited the mess bar at Aldergrove, spent most of his spare time in his room crocheting. He could make the most beautiful garments – most I think were crocheted dresses for his wife back home in England.

But it was fun to know you could slip into civilian life and whether the IRA boys were fooled or not, they always left us alone. I never felt any strong affiliation towards either camp. I was too busy enjoying myself both professionally and privately to be too concerned about why I was there at all. I was in my late twenties and political issues were for knackered old shits, not the lads. Paul O'Brennan was one such legend in his own drinking time. He was my deputy flight commander and one of the few who could out drink me. He would be in the bar every night long after everyone else had given up but he was also the first in work the following morning. He smoked like a chimney, drank like a fish and anything in a skirt he considered to be fair game. Paul was a demon squash player who also enjoyed a hand of bridge. There is no doubt that he burned the candle at both ends and in the middle. Paul O'Brennan died of a massive heart attack before reaching his thirty-fifth birthday. I dare say he wouldn't have changed a single second of it either.

Suffice it to say that some very colourful characters served their time on detachment in Northern Ireland. There was one guy who insisted on turning up in the officers' mess in the most outrageous kit. He was a navigator called Mick Geoghan and he was an incredible eccentric. His favourite outfit was a canary yellow suit which he would wear in the mess after 7p.m. at night when we were expected to conform to the jacket and tie rule. About six months later he went back to the same tailor and ordered a lime green suit. One night a more senior officer finally lost his rag and ordered Geoghan to change into something better than that 'damned yellow outfit'. Mick promptly disappeared to his room and returned in his latest lime green creation . . . He was banned from the bar but, undaunted, Mick set up a bar in his own room where he could wear anything he wanted to. We often popped in for a drink wearing anything from jeans and a T-shirt to a towelling robe having just stepped from the shower.

Despite the rules we shipped in girls of every religious denomination, creed and colour. The girls from Stormont were very regular guests at Aldergrove. Many of us firmly believed the rules were only there to be broken. It would have been rude not to. The boys had only one rule that must be obeyed: to notch up a £100 bar bill and complete 100 hours flying in the Province as quickly as possible.

One of the most regular tasks we undertook was vehicle checking. We would spot a vehicle that either looked or was reported to us as suspicious and we would chase it down the road landing about a mile ahead. There the troops we had in the back of the Wessex would bundle out to stop the car and check its occupants. There was also the night tasking when we would drop a stick of troops in a field somewhere in South Armagh. They would stay out for four or five days living in hedgerows, simply monitoring what was happening in the area. When we were tasked to pick them up again we would groan at the prospect. We probably didn't need to locate them by map – we could smell them a mile away!

There were many incidents and outrages that are both too numerous to mention and too commonplace for everyone who lives or has worked in Northern Ireland. As an apolitical animal I could still see that there was an appalling division of spoils between the Catholics and the Protestants. Catholic areas were by far the most run down and areas like the Divis Flats were on a par with some of the most atrocious ghettos orchestrated by Nazi Germany. There were times, however, when a particular atrocity or other horrified me so much that I tried to erase the incident from my mind.

In the early summer of 1978 I had been tasked to fly into South Armagh. The location was another anonymous green field. The Army were already there; often we did not know the precise details of their activities. A cordon had been placed along both sides of a boundary hedge. We had been asked to fly in with replacement troops.

Our golden rule was never to leave the Wessex on the ground for more seconds than was absolutely necessary – we were such obvious sitting ducks. But when we landed the troops we replaced pointed out to us precisely what they had been guarding on the ground. In the hedge, quite open to view, was the body of a very small child, I think not more than a year old. It had remained untouched by the Army and would stay there until the bomb disposal boys were available to deal with it.

It was not unheard of that a child or young teenage girl would be kidnapped – by the provos – to be dumped in a hedgerow for the British Army to find. I later discovered that when this baby was finally removed its stomach was found to be packed with explosives. Pictures were taken at the time of the discovery of the baby, all pretty sickening. But the parents were not informed of what had happened to their child – the baby was missing, presumed dead. Such appalling incidents were not uncommon. Now, as I scour my log book for details of that shocking event I can find no mention of it. I know roughly when it happened but I failed to log that flying task as anything more than routine. I am also aware of an incident at Newtonhamilton in South Armagh where a Protestant activist was taken after capture by the IRA and subsequently tortured for information. A doctor was brought in to the staunchly Republican town having been recruited to carry out the job. The victim was actually skinned alive by the doctor and was kept alive throughout his torture in a bid to glean information from him. This grisly story very quickly filtered through to the officers' mess at Aldergrove.

On the morning of 16 December 1979, just nine days before Christmas, I wasn't expecting to be home until the middle of January, and work for the next few weeks at least was the only thing on the agenda. Although married, I was still not a dad and had volunteered myself over the festive season to give the crews with children a chance to celebrate Christmas with their young ones. We had been tasked on that cold, dank morning to carry out a VCP – vehicle check point. The idea is to saturate the area on the ground with troops for a brief period of time.

We flew the troops into an area just outside Dungannon – a small town on the western shores of Loch Neagh. There were eight soldiers in two patrols of four and we flew them in fast and low in the Wessex in leap-frog fashion. This way four soldiers are flown in by air, then a Land Rover waiting nearby pulls up containing the other four. We drop off our four, pick up the four from the vehicle and fly them on to another road junction in the area.

The operation barely lasted more than an hour but the complete saturation means that it is unlikely for any vehicle in the region to escape the Army's notice. During my time in Northern Ireland we picked up some thoroughly nasty individuals on the Army's wanted list this way. In fact we carried out this particular type of operation with a good deal of success but inevitably the courts let most of these terrorists free within a matter of days.

So close to Christmas, even the prospect of spending it on duty in Northern Ireland failed to dampen our spirits. The locals were doing their best to make the lives of the servicemen considerably more pleasant. There were food parcels, videos and the odd bottle which always came with a thank you note for our efforts in helping to keep the peace. There was quite a jolly air about the bases. We'd even decorated the inside of our helicopter cabin with fairy lights and we played carols over the intercom. While we got on with the job, we tried to make it as painless as possible. And there was no question that our lives in the air were considerably better than that of the average soldier probably stuck for days in some bleak bog in South Armagh. It would only be fair to admit that we had all the glamour and little of the pain. But as ever, the lottery of life is always ready to play its ace of spades.

As I transitioned away from having dropped four troops off there was a blinding flash. It was all around us and the helicopter shook uncontrollably for what seemed like an eternity. Frantically, I checked the controls trying to work out what had happened. Whatever it was seemed to be happening in slow motion and I had no control over it. We had just dropped off the four soldiers down to a waiting Land Rover on their way to the next VCP location. Moments later their vehicle drove over a land mine and there were four more British soldiers who would not be celebrating Christmas that year.

Through the bright orange flash and the smoke I had seen jagged pieces of metal and canvas come cartwheeling across the sky. Most of it went into a tree. I thanked God that the four soldiers we had just exchanged for the victims in the Land Rover could not see from their seats in the back of the aircraft what had just happened to their mates.

I shall never cease to be amazed by how the military training machine suddenly takes over at times when sheer blind panic would seem more appropriate. I heard myself calmly calling on the radio: 'Hello zero, whisky juliet, contact.' That last word immediately alerted operations to the fact that we had come under fire. I wanted to ask why and felt an urge to strike out in retaliation. But that calming military influence simply assumes control, telling you what you must do. Instead, there was a steady voice on the radio speaking clearly to the ops over the airwaves. We flew back to Dungannon and en route explained in more detail what had happened out there. And while you know what you saw, the memory quickly begins to play tricks on the mind. There is always the hope that those soldiers had not made it to the Land Rover and had missed the blast.

We landed back at company headquarters waiting for a rescue force to be hastily put together in the bleak hope of finding any survivors. But terrorist organisations in Northern Ireland were very good at initiating a come-on. They can deftly create an incident such as the one we had witnessed in the sure knowledge that it would draw even larger number of troops into the same area. And that's when the real killing would take place.

This was always the sickening end of the job. You would fly back hoping to pick up survivors. Often they were injured and you would move heaven and earth to get to them. If they were already dead they could wait until modern combat technology decided the area was safe enough to go into. Only then would the dead be picked up to be sent home for a decent burial. We flew back, not looking for survivors but to confirm that the number of corpses matched up with the troops we had earlier dropped off there. And it is no good finding a hand or a foot, that soldier could have survived and still be alive somewhere. But a headless corpse hanging from a tree is not a pretty sight.

On the way back to Aldergrove we stopped at Omagh to refuel. As we completed the refuelling, Cy Rodgers, the crewman, and I were walking across the parade ground when we heard a voice repeatedly scream out to us: 'Staff sergeant'. We ignored it until we heard a military clicking of heels rapidly approaching us from behind. As we turned we were confronted by a rather red-faced major from the local regiment. He looked at Cy and said: 'Staff sergeant, I was calling you,' to which Cy replied: 'I am an RAF flight sergeant and not an Army staff sergeant.'

The now somewhat perplexed major replied: 'Well, if you had been in the Army you would have been a staff sergeant.'

Cy looked him squarely in the eye before calmly answering, 'Sir, if I had been in the Army I would have been a fucking brigadier!'

That Christmas Day was one of mixed fortunes for me. In fact it was to be a Christmas when I very nearly cooked my own goose. We had been flying vehicle check-points with the duty detachment commander, a squadron leader senior to myself. I'd been flying the Wessex for a good few years and my posting to Hong Kong was almost in the bag. My first child was due to be born and I was very confident about myself and my skills.

We were chasing a car which had broken through a border patrol close to Crossmaglen and we had driven it very near to the border with Eire. I ran in alongside it on a fairly straight stretch of road with hedges either side. I pushed the car off the road with the main wheel of the helicopter. My co-pilot just sat there with his mouth open, never uttering a word. Although he was a senior officer, he was not fully experienced with operations in Northern Ireland which was very lucky for me. As the car tumbled off the road and into a field, soldiers waiting nearby ran to pick up the occupants. It transpired that a known terrorist was inside the car and he was about to spend the rest of

Christmas Day staring at the four walls of a prison cell. I really was beginning to feel rather pleased with myself.

It was 25 December and even the air traffic control team at Aldergrove were enjoying the day off. It was the only day we were given a free range to get in and out of the airfield under our own steam. The main runway is used by incoming airliners and looking down it from a panoramic window in the officers' mess there is a beautiful view out to the north. I knew that a number of my colleagues would be in that mess bar enjoying the festive spirit. Full of my own high spirits I flew in from the north straight towards that window just as fast as I could go, probably at about 120mph. As we came over the perimeter fence of the airfield at no more than four feet above it, I dropped the Wessex down even further and flew straight at this ground-floor window of the officers' mess.

By this stage my co-pilot had decided he'd had enough and prepared to take control of the aircraft, but I had the bit between my teeth and, despite the fact that he was my senior, it was my day. I informed him that if he touched the controls I would bite his hands off. I continued to fly at that window before pulling up at the very last moment as I prepared to perform a wing-over around the top of the officers' mess building. I had left it almost too late; as I pulled up over the building I lifted my backside as far as I could off my seat as I strained to get the aircraft further away from the building. I pulled very hard and then felt a resounding thump.

Fairly chastened, I landed the helicopter and above the noise of the two Rolls Royce engines my deputy detachment commander, my co-pilot, was screaming his lungs out at me. I had a quick look around the aircraft and there wasn't a scratch on it; whatever we had hit had taken a bashing from the tail wheel.

We walked into the operation room for debriefing where I spent some considerable time being informed by a squadron leader that my days in the RAF were numbered. He was calmed down by the ops officer who told him that there had been a phone call from the Commander of the Armed Forces Northern Ireland. He had heard of our incursion along the border and how a Wessex pilot had physically pushed the Ford Escort off the road. The message was that whoever had flown that manoeuvre should be recommended for a medal. My flight commander informed me that I was the luckiest bastard alive and that my outrageous antics on return to Aldergrove had just been cancelled out by the commendation from the Army's Commander.

A day or so later I discovered what we had hit with the tail wheel. I found three ridge tiles on the ground outside the officers' mess. I managed to force my way into the Department of Environment building on the base as the staff were away for the holiday. From there I borrowed a bucket, some new tiles and sufficient cement. I scaled the officers' mess and discreetly replaced the roof tiles. To this day I don't think anyone knows what I did.

One of our favourite and highly illicit excursions mostly took place on a Sunday. A Wessex would be tasked on patrol every other day of the week, but Sunday was a perfect time to indulge in a little 'church wazzing'. As the faithful flocked to morning service we would swoop in on the terrified congregation. The game was to get as close as you could to the church roof without displacing a tile.

A couple of years before, in fact it was in May 1977, undercover soldier Robert Nairac had been captured by the IRA who brutally tortured him before murdering him. Captain Nairac was a fine young man, a Grenadier Guard I both knew and respected. The intelligence information filtering back to us painted a gruesome picture of his treatment at the hands of his captors. We were all smarting at his death and revenge was not far from the minds of many of us. I shall never forget the very next time I had a chance to indulge in a spot of church wazzing. This time it was a Wednesday but, unusually for midweek, there was a flock of worshippers gathering outside the church just down the road from the Three Steps Inn in the village of Drumintee, South Armagh, where the captain had been kidnapped only a week before.

It was 10.30a.m. as we pulled up and winged over the gathering crowd. I think I could only have been a foot or so from the roof of the church. It was so close we thought we had better return to check for structural damage. Minutes after our attack, there was no sign of the little crowd who earlier had gathered outside. The cars were gone and there was nothing to suggest life of any kind. But lying there in the road was a coffin. It had been abandoned by the terrified mourners and pallbearers and its occupant was patiently awaiting a decent burial.

Support Helicopter Detachment in Northern Ireland rescued a goat from the Army Air Corps base at Long Kesh. He was there to keep the grass tidy but he became something of a celebrity among the air crews. The goat, whose name was Paddy McGinty, had a notoriously vicious streak. We put this down to him being forced to eat the grass around the helicopter landing pads at Long Kesh. It must have been like living inside a huge concrete mixer that was going night and day. No wonder the goat was permanently in a bad mood. We decided that it was time to rescue the goat from his torture and take him to the relative peace at Aldergrove. He was duly collected and flown to Aldergrove in the back of a Wessex. It was funny how no one at Long Kesh seemed to object to his removal. The plan was to allow him to graze around the officers' mess where it would again be his job to keep the grass down.

At the time we had an adjutant on detachment called Stuart Nuttall. Amazingly he had spent some time before joining the Air Force as a goatherd, and from the day he confessed this interesting detail he was forever known as Goatherd Nuttall. He was the ideal man to take care of our new arrival. Sadly Paddy McGinty never lost his vicious streak, in fact I think it got steadily worse.

On evenings when the mess bar was particularly full someone would decide that it was time to bring in Paddy. The results were always devastating. The place was trashed by Paddy on a fairly regular basis. Chairs, tables, endless glasses would be brought crashing to the floor by his determined headbutting. The bar would be soaked in beer as Paddy butted into the furniture or when individuals, trying desperately to avoid his lethal horns, would crash into a table sending it flying. McGinty was a terror and there was no escape from his evil attacks. He was actually terrified of the dark and it was the only time you could persuade him to stay in his pen – a large upended packing crate with a door cut out at the side.

Of course as we flew tasks on a twenty-four-hour basis the crews could be sleeping in their rooms at any time of night or day. That was when some wag would drag Paddy by his collar shoving him into some slumbering officer's room before closing the door and legging it down the corridor. Paddy behaved like a goat possessed. He would crash around the twelve-foot-square room, terrified of the dark and panicking because he could not retire to the safety of his packing crate. It became a real skill to rise from the bed and attempt to find the light switch without being attacked by Paddy. The room was always wrecked and the officer concerned usually ended up severely bruised and beaten by the marauding goat. Finally, to give his victims a fighting chance, we painted Paddy's horns a dayglo red.

We ran out of ideas about what to do with Paddy and in the end we gave him to a farmer. Some months later I flew down to the farm just to see how Paddy was getting on. The farmer came out to meet us and he was full of apologies. 'The goat,' he explained, 'has sadly passed away. But you can still come and see him if you want to.'

He invited us into his sitting room and there was our Paddy stretched out in front of the fire, a rather splendid hearthrug.

During our operations in Northern Ireland we were regularly tasked to assist the Army during some engagement or other with the terrorists. One such incident took place in 1979 when we were called to give assistance to troops involved in a fire fight near to Warrenpoint. Later that year in the August, Warrenpoint was to become the scene of the most appalling carnage resulting in the death of nineteen people. Sixteen Parachute Regiment soldiers and one civilian were killed in a Bank Holiday ambush on the Irish border. Two massive booby trap bomb blasts claimed the lives of the paratroopers as they drove past in a lorry and a Land Rover. It was a terrible act of revenge; the IRA blamed the Parachute Regiment for the 'Bloody Sunday' killings in Londonderry seven years before. Now they were exacting payment in full.

On the night we were tasked into South Armagh there was plenty of action. I was flying with Mike Buckland and as we approached the area we could see plenty of tracer being fired. The engagement lasted about fifteen minutes and you could see the tracer arcing through the night sky as it ricocheted off the surrounding buildings.

It was a spectacular scene but in the middle of all this mayhem was a small bungalow with all its lights on and an elderly lady standing by the sitting room window in order to get a good view of what was going on. We screamed from the open door of the Wessex to get down under a table out of the way but she waved and carried on enjoying this rather dangerous non-spectator sport. As she watched several bullets bounced off the roof of her bungalow while others clanged against the guttering. It was horrible for us as we could see that she would almost certainly be killed if a bullet smashed through her window.

As the gunfire died down we quickly moved in and picked up the patrol to whisk them away to safety. None of them had been hurt and they were all high on the experience of exchanging fire with the 'enemy'. Days later I ventured back to the area. I had not stopped thinking about that old lady and I hoped that she had not been hurt. Thankfully she was safe and sound but when I tried to explain to her the dangers of what she had done that night she said: 'Didn't you realise that I was safe? I had the double glazing installed only three months ago.'

6

28 Squadron, Hong Kong – 1980 to 1982

I was posted to Hong Kong almost by default. During the final months of my tour on 72 Squadron I had played off my skills as a helicopter pilot against my social indiscretions. Getting drunk, falling over, blowing up messes and being thoroughly irresponsible, that is unless I was on the flight deck of a helicopter, were par for the course I had laid out for myself. It was a metaphorical bank account where the credits were built up by specific requests for my skills and the debits were a pair of badly singed station commander's trousers, or something equally as ridiculous.

About seven months before I was due for posting from 72 Squadron, Wing Commander Tony Ryles summoned me for interview and reminded me that the normal procedure was for an officer to make three choices for his next posting. Subject to the requirements of the service and the availability of the choices, you tended to get what you'd asked for. If you wanted to enjoy a few years on exchange with the Army or the Navy you could or if you fancied life as an instructor you could. Some people opted for search and rescue and other guys tried to get a transfer onto transport aircraft.

But I didn't fancy an exchange to the Army or Navy because I'd already spent over two out of three years away from home on detachment in Northern Ireland. Sheila was expecting our first child and I wanted to be with her. I certainly didn't want to teach. For one thing, the Royal Air Force Central Flying School was the most antique organisation you could imagine. It was full of self-important and self-protecting individuals, many of whom wouldn't have lasted two minutes on a modern-day flying squadron.

One of the chief helicopter examiners for the Air Force was kicking and screaming after being posted to a front-line helicopter squadron. And no wonder, within a week of starting his operational conversion training on the twin-engine Wessex he was thrown out, incapable of making the grade.

Funny thing was that many years later I witnessed exactly the same thing while on Tornados. Again there was a hopelessly inadequate Tornado flying instructor who had been posted to XV Squadron in Germany. He was a thoroughly nice guy and quite a reasonable pilot but flying a modern-day aeroplane has to be second nature. It is being able to operate it that keeps you alive. But he was eventually posted from the squadron after about eighteen months. You were supposed to be able to make a contribution to the squadron after about four months. Here he was after nearly five times that period of time still struggling. He was posted to do a job on the ground.

I met him a couple of years later while he was on a visit back to Germany examining our pilots in their competence to fly the Tornado! At the time I was the training officer on the squadron and he and I had a discreet little chat along the lines that he wasn't going to fly with any of our pilots and the Central Flying School had better send out someone else – capable of doing the job. The service is full of examples like that. It's never what you know but who and it is not what you do, just the way you carry it out. There is a tradition in the Air Force, even today, where you cannot say the initials QFI – Qualified Flying Instructor – without gritting your teeth and spitting between the 'Q' and the 'F'.

But back to Tony Ryles. He told me quite clearly that he had changed the tradition of three choices of posting. There was to be his choice, or mine. He told me that if for the remaining months of my tour on the squadron I behaved, then within reason I could have my choice of posting. Of course, should I stray from the straight and narrow just one more time, then I would have his choice of posting. And he told me what his choice of posting would be. I'd be off to languish for the next two or three years in some HQ building in a dusty office full of paperwork. He explained that he would make sure I'd spend that time working as close as possible to aeroplanes without there ever being a chance of flying one.

It sounded worse than death. It goes without saying that I tried to be a model of propriety for the remainder of my time on the squadron. I did behave and was careful not to get caught out for any minor misdemeanour that would have clipped my wings. I also tried to keep as many miles as I could between me and the squadron commander. If he was in Northern Ireland I did my best to remain at Odiham, just in case my devil's horns popped out at the wrong moment.

My first choice of posting was to go back to fighter training. The Jaguar at the time was in the same group as the Wessex Force – number 38 group within the structure of strike command. I think he raised his eyebrows at this request. He was a career officer and I'd had a very good first tour from a flying point of view. I'd already been recognised as a very capable aviator and my professional accomplishments had already put me head and shoulders above many others. In his eyes the smart career move was either to stay on helicopters and join the management structure or volunteer for a ground posting in order to progress up through the ranks.

He believed, as many others did, that if I could temper my enthusiasm to be a social hand grenade I could make it to the top.

But the idea of controlling my own corridor of power was abhorrent to me. I had joined the Air Force to fly and I eventually left after eighteen years knowing little else. By my reckoning, because the Jaguar was in the same group, the squadron commander might have some sway to get me a posting. A few months later during one of our regular progress meetings, Wing Commander Ryles told me that it looked as though I might get a second bite of the cherry.

But when I thought about it at length I concluded that I would stay on helicopters and try for a posting either to Hong Kong or Cyprus. The simple facts were that a transfer to Jaguars would mean at least two years of frustration and damned hard work, neither of which I particularly enjoyed. Also, I was beginning to get responsible. It wasn't anything that the Air Force had done. It was because I was about to become a father and I owed it to Sheila and our unborn child to bring a bit of stability into my own life and the lives of those dear to me.

So I went to see Wing Commander Ryles and asked

to go to 28 Squadron Hong Kong. At the time I thought it was probably the last opportunity I would have to fly a high-performance fighter and I believed I had just said goodbye to that chance. My future lay in flying the trusty Wessex on which I had already clocked up over a thousand flying hours.

The wing commander's first reaction verged on fury. He'd obviously spent a lot of hours and called in as many favours as he could to get me cross-rolled onto fast jets but even then I saw through his ire. He was angry because he wanted me to know how much now wasted work he had put in but I think he was also secretly pleased that I'd made the right choice in his mind. Not only was I giving my family a bit of priority which hitherto I hadn't done at all, but I was also making the right career move.

By early 1980 confirmation of my posting to Hong Kong came and I was expecting to go out in the early spring. But I think at that stage the most important thing on my mind was Sheila and her bump. My son, Michael, was born on 29 February at 9.18p.m. and he was six weeks old when we flew from Gatwick on a British Airtours Boeing 707 to Kaytak airport in Kowloon, Hong Kong.

I recall that we stopped to refuel on the way at Dubai in the Middle East. All I can remember is that refuelling took longer than expected and the air conditioning on board began to falter. The inside of the aeroplane got hotter and hotter. It was a dry heat, not terribly uncomfortable, but at this late stage I began to wonder what the climate in Hong Kong would be like.

At the top of the aircraft steps on arrival at Hong Kong's airport it was like being hit in the face by a 30mph tea cloth which had just been dipped in boiling water. We were to get used to the heat and humidity because the ministry in its wisdom had provided us with a spacious apartment with no hint of air conditioning but with ceiling fans which looked and operated as though they had come out of the ark.

In those days, a posting to Hong Kong was regarded as a real peach of a job. The flying was challenging and the perks were second to none. Allowances could almost double your salary and even our humble flight lieutenant's apartment could have housed the entire squadron. One of the perks on arrival was that you spent four days acclimatising at a luxury hotel in the centre of Kowloon. By the time my posting had come to an end that little treat was already history. The chaps who arrived later with their families moved straight into their accommodation saying hello and goodbye to the people they were replacing quite literally on the doorstep.

One of the last things I had done before leaving Blighty was to sell the car. It was a sporty chocolate brown Lancia with ivory leather upholstery and the chap I sold it to was so concerned about my sense of loss that he paid me the £2,000 in cash and then allowed me to keep the car the remaining two days until we left the country. His kindness allowed me to part with my pride and joy almost on the apron at Gatwick airport. I converted the cash into Hong Kong dollars, tucking the brightly coloured notes into my wallet for immediate spending money on arrival in the Far East. The trouble was I had no idea of the exchange rate or the particular value of each note. I didn't care either, I just wanted to have fun and in my book that includes spending money. However, the waiter in the bar at our temporary five-star home thought his luck was in when I handed him a note worth £1,000 (HK$10,000) to pay for a round of drinks, especially when I casually turned to my drinking partner, Flight Lieutenant Barrie Simmonds, asking if I should tell the waiter to keep the change. 'I don't think so, old boy,' he replied. 'You've just given him nearly a thousand quid for two gin and tonics!'

Of course it was after an appalling incident in Germany a couple of years before that Barrie and I had been warned we would never serve on the same squadron again. The unfortunate event had resulted in an officers' mess being blown up and a nearby rockery converted to a fishpond with the aid of several ounces of plastic explosive. We were certainly banged to rights and bollocked at the subsequent trial but thankfully the RAF has an extremely short memory and here we were in Honkers sharing a drink.

Going back to when we first arrived in Hong Kong the driving standards I noted were appalling, so in order to give myself and my family the best possible protection I bought the biggest car I could afford, an Australian Ford Falcon. I am six feet one inch tall and I could lie right across the front seats without touching either door, it was a monster. I paid £2,000 for it and two years later, with so many dents and bashes, it wasn't even worth the bus fare to the airport. But it had certainly accounted for a good few Japanese cars along the way.

The only modification I had done to the car was to have the chromium fenders replaced with rigid steel joists. My favourite trick if anyone annoyed me by driving too close behind was to slam on the brakes and as they crashed into my heavy-duty bumpers I would pull away and drive off, leaving the unfortunate motorist behind to survey the wreckage of his car.

Some of the Air Force advice on how to cope with acclimatisation was to sleep only when really tired and to try to cross the eight-hour barrier that you had just flown through by keeping going while awake. Of course, your body clock is telling you all the time that you should be in bed when everyone around you is rushing off to work.

There are all sorts of things to say about Hong Kong. There was the extraordinary censorship to start with. Any hint of complete nudity would be torn from magazines on sale regardless of whether an article on the next page was left making any sense or not. But the Chinese would not bat an eyelid at stomach churning pictures of headless corpses in the newspapers.

It is an amazing place from a military point of view. There is an area slightly bigger than the Isle of Wight with the population of London and life never stops to take a breath. When I was there the concentration of troops was larger than anywhere else on earth during peacetime. Also, there was a mixture of the most modern technology available with the quaint traditions of the British Empire under Queen Victoria.

There was *HMS Tamar*, the nerve centre of the British Forces in Hong Kong. It was a tower block right on the waterfront of Hong Kong Island with state of the art communications equipment and all the central operations desks at hand. It was exactly as you would imagine a high-tech control centre to be. You could be talking to the person at the next desk and then with a push of a button discussing tactics with a colleague in Washington, America.

And yet only a few miles away from this place was Gun Club, the home of the United Services Recreation Club with its palms, manicured lawns and dozens of servants in immaculate white uniforms, the sort with polished brass buttons at the neck. It was the last days of the Empire. There were beautiful white colonial style buildings with shallow sloping roofs, endless balconies and louvred shutters. A punkah wallah would not have been out of place standing on the polished parquet floors. The contrast was tangible. It was like enjoying all the tastes, smells and sights that Hong Kong could provide all at once. The other thing that was very apparent was the power the military quite clearly had. We were almost totally immune to the law, which was handy for me, and we were treated with respect bordering on reverence.

I started flying training at the end of May 1980. There were several new skills to learn as the squadron had a search and rescue role in addition to supporting the Army. While I was well versed in Army support techniques I'd still had much to learn. For a start hovering over the water at the controls of a Wessex was something I had always found incredibly difficult. It is a taxing skill to muster in any event but for me it was definitely an Achilles' heel. It was also something that I had studiously avoided. Other flying skills came easily to me and I hated the idea of being shown up because I could not master this one basic technique.

Early training involved winching volunteers from the decks of Hong Kong police launches. I felt sorry for the poor bastards as I bounced them off the sides of the deck on countless occasions. It surprised me that there was never any shortage of volunteers.

Another training method we practised for work over the sea was using a brightly dayglo-painted five-gallon oil drum which had a weighted fin welded to one end and two hoops to the other. This would be thrown into the sea and then we would fly a circuit around it and retrieve it using a hook attached to the winch cable. This was known as wet drum winching. The dayglo drum was always known as 'the survivor' and the hook was 'the winchman'. In reality we were practising how to pluck human beings from the water.

The normal helicopter crew would be a pilot and navigator cum winch operator and the winchman. In simple terms the pilot made all the decisions and got all the blame, the winch operator gave all the directions and got all the credit while the winchman dangled on the end of the wire and got all the medals. It certainly made good sense to practise with a hook and a five-gallon drum before subjecting human beings to my own cack-handed attempts. During my early efforts to lift the drum out of the water I ran out of fuel and ideas and abandoned the drum to its own devices as it floated out into the South China Sea.

As time progressed and my skills developed it became one of the most satisfying flying accomplishments. It is a very co-ordinated exercise – as you run into this pinprick floating on the sea you may only get a brief glimpse every ten or fifteen seconds as it dodges between the waves, and for the last twenty or so yards you can no longer see it at all as it lies vertically beneath the aircraft. It can only be described as a sort of aerial ballet. In the final stages of lifting an object from the water it is no longer good enough to be yards or only feet from the target. You have to fly to near inch-perfect accuracy and in rough water with strong winds when it is all going well it is the nearest thing I can imagine to an out of body experience.

The winch operator's patter is incessant with his directions of forward or up and down, right and left, and almost before you can mentally react to those instructions to move the aircraft a few inches your body seems to have complied with that request. Sometimes you could be hovering at forty knots because of the winds and tide. The mission was to position yourself twenty feet vertically above whatever it was you wanted to lift, and it wasn't just a case of being able to stay there long enough to put in a hook and lift away because what you were practising for was maybe the day when the winchman had to cut a victim free from a yacht's rigging or parachute cords or any other manner of entanglement. This meant hovering with total accuracy for several minutes or however long it took to free that person.

It seemed necessary to me to remain ignorant of the power I held. Just one muscular twitch of the finger on the collective lever could mean life or death. A taut winch cable moved just a foot in the wrong direction can cut a person in half.

For me the biggest eye-opener of my tour there was the night flying. Hong Kong is a colony made up of a peninsular and dozens of islands, many of them inhabited. One of the jobs we had was to be on hand to go anywhere at any time to fly sick or injured people to hospital in Kowloon. Various procedural techniques had been developed over the years to get into various landing sites. Some of them were hairy enough by day let alone in the dead of night. It was darker than night itself and at times trickier than a boatload of monkeys.

Less than a month after arriving in the colony the alarm bells rang and we were asked to scramble a Wessex to go in search for a civilian helicopter which it was believed had crashed on a nearby hillside. It had been a particularly stormy and choppy day and for some reason troops were thin on the ground. The majority of air crew were already either out on duties or training. By the time the station medical officer had arrived the squadron commander, Squadron Leader Malcolm Pledger, was starting up an aircraft, Flight Lieutenant Geoff Clark was to be the winchman and I was to be the winch operator.

It didn't take us long to find the crash site. The aircraft had been taking in supplies to construction workers who were installing pylons and power cables. It seems that a cargo net suspended beneath a Llama single-engine four-seater helicopter had become entangled in the tail rotor sending the aircraft plummeting to the ground.

The scramble message had already told us that we were looking for two occupants and from a stand-off position I could see that one of them was certainly not going to enjoy teatime because he was spread all over what was left of the instrument panel. But the pilot of the shattered aircraft was lying face down clear of the wreckage and it seemed as though he had gone straight through the perspex canopy. He appeared to be moving and did not seem to be too badly injured. It became a priority to get to him. The aircraft had gone down in trees and in the final stages of the crash the rotor had hacked away its own small clearing in the jungle.

It was my turn to be the winch operator while Geoff Clark fastened himself and the doctor into the winchman's harness. I talked Squadron Leader Pledger into position over the crash site and as we paid out winch cable with Geoff and the doctor on it, we climbed steadily so as to minimise the disruption caused by our own rotor blades. As soon as Geoff and the doctor reached the ground they released themselves from the harness and I began to retract the winch cable as we flew away. We flew in a wide circle around the site and waited for either a hand or smoke signal from Geoff calling us back in.

Geoff was a seasoned veteran in the skills of search and rescue. He had been based on several of the UK SAR squadrons and had seen and done most of it dozens of times before. Initially because we hadn't been called back in straightaway it seemed to us that there may have been some hope for the pilot. What we didn't know was that the doctor was fairly inexperienced. Geoff had already taken one look at the pilot and knew that he was dead but the doctor insisted on attempting resuscitation. He was lying face down and Geoff saw immediately that the body was over seven feet tall. He was intact but everything else was shattered. Any muscular twitching we may or may not have seen had taken place after the soul had already left the body.

Some twenty minutes later we picked up Geoff and the doctor and flew back to Sek Kong. For the rest of the day our task was to fly in and around the crash scene. The rules are that nothing can be moved until photographed from every angle for the investigators in the hope that any tiny shred of evidence can be used to prevent a similar tragedy.

But human life was not always treated with such respect. It wasn't to be long before I learned that colour and creed has a great bearing on simple worth.

Two months after my arrival I was well into theatre conversion and had been flying intensive day operations. However, night flying in Hong Kong was still a black art and according to the rule book, while I had done a little night training, I was still not allowed to be aircraft captain during the hours of darkness. There is an interesting entry in my flying log book on 27 July 1980. It records one hour and fifteen minutes of daylight flying even though the vast majority of that time was spent under the cover of darkness. I was duty pilot during the day and was about to be relieved by one of the more experience Hong Kong flyers when the scramble bell rang out and within minutes I was airborne and westbound towards the Mai Po marshes. My crew were Master Air Loadmaster Tony Rodmell, the equivalent to a warrant officer and the most senior non-commissioned rank, and the winchman was Sergeant Howard Jones.

A border patrol had spotted a group of IIs – illegal immigrants. The Mai Po marshes were a favourite crossing point for illegals from mainland China and a popular time to cross was at last light. This really was a game of Russian roulette because if they weren't clear of the marsh area and onto solid land by the time it was completely dark then they would almost certainly be taken out to sea with the rising tide. Too early they would be picked up by the eagle-eyed border patrols and too late they would end up in Davy Jones's locker.

There were two kinds of illegal immigrant when it came to a helicopter flight: those who ran towards you when you approached them because they thought you were going to fly them to the gold-paved streets they dreamed of; and those who ran away, probably because they thought you were some kind of airborne dragon about to devour them. This particular group that we had been scrambled to intercept was the latter.

By the time we got to the marshes we were well into twilight and unlike the half-darkness we know in Britain it tends to be either day or night; light or dark in the Tropics. Those poor bastards were fleeing away from us in every and any direction. They were hiding under mangrove, sometimes neck deep in a black oily soup; a mixture of mud and seawater. We hovered with the main wheels of the aircraft almost touching the surface of the swamps and Tony and Howard simply leant out of the aircraft door, picked them up by the scruff of the neck and threw them into the back of the helicopter. Within days they would be back in China undergoing some form of 'therapy' to make sure they never attempted to cross from communism into capitalism again.

We had caught about seven or eight of the terrified group still rushing in all directions but rapidly tiring. By now I was having to use the aircraft landing light to search them out from under the mangrove canopy. The landing light on the Wessex is a kind of gimballed affair which you can swing in any direction desired and it was proving most valuable at the time. We were running very short of fuel by the time it was pitch dark and there were still four or five people to pick up. Being so low on fuel I had a decision to make. It was either to leave them and forget them knowing nothing this side of life would ever see them again or risk our necks picking up what would certainly be dead bodies and beyond any help in this life. There is no doubt that Jones, Rodmell or myself would be the last to see them alive and at the outside they had about fifty minutes to live before the night-covered tide would sweep them into the sea.

A refuel would take about half an hour at least. We called up on the HF radio that we would require a rotor's running refuel. The refuelling operators would duck under the rotor blades as soon as our wheels touched the ground, and just as soon as we had enough fuel on board to complete the task in hand we would be up and away rounding up the stragglers back in the marshes.

As we lifted away from Sek Kong I received over the radio a direct order to return to base. The reason was that I had not been formally credited with the required qualification to fly as aircraft captain at night in Hong Kong. It didn't matter that I'd flown dozens of operational hours at night over Northern Ireland, it just mattered that some stupid half-wit in his tower of power could see that the rules were obeyed to the letter regardless of the sense in it. Someone was trying to persuade me that the slight bending of a rule was a much bigger crime than letting half a dozen or so human beings drown.

It was a sickening sensation for me to become painfully aware that the person giving me that order would almost certainly have risked life during a search and rescue operation back in the United Kingdom and yet several Chinese lives could be thrown away in order to comply with bureaucracy. Anyway, it didn't take me long to decide what to do. To have handed the aircraft over to a Hong Kong night-qualified pilot would have taken too long and be too late. What's more, I knew where those terrified people were. I chose to ignore the instruction and Howard and Tony were with me all the way.

We rushed back out to the marshes but by now the tide was well up and the people were wallowing in the water. I felt like a big benevolent fisherman as Tony and Howard were grabbing them and throwing them down the back of the helicopter just as quickly as they could. My estimation of the numbers had been well out and by the time we did our last recce around the marshes to make sure there was no one left to perish out there that night, there were twenty-four people on the helicopter. Three crew and twenty-one Chinese, including a couple of kids. They were huddled down at the back, cold, wet, terrified and tired but at least they were alive.

I landed back at base well into the night and the

boss was absolutely livid. He was apoplectic with rage. It didn't matter that we'd brought nearly two dozen people to safety from a certain watery grave. It only mattered that I'd broken the rules; how dare I? I was left in no doubt that the book was going to be thrown at me. However, I filled in the aircraft's technical log and signed the authorisation sheets to record the flight for posterity. I logged the time flying in the daytime column of the flight authorisation sheets. I'd had my bollocking and the boss had left, by the time I saw him again next morning there was nothing more he could do. All records of that flight show it was conducted entirely by day and therefore perfectly legitimate. The job is only ever finished when the paperwork is done.

I was faintly uneasy about the political set up in Hong Kong and my role in it. At one time illegal immigrants from communist China had been welcomed as successful escapees from a repressive regime. After a while the 'touchbase policy' came into effect. This meant that if an illegal immigrant could walk into a police station or military depot without detection then they would be issued with Hong Kong residency papers and become legalised citizens on the spot. It was a glorified game of tag. Caught outside the copshop and you were repatriated for a good hiding and yet inside the station you would be home and dry.

All that had changed by the time I arrived out there, when an illegal immigrant was just that and could be sent back at any time. In fact shortly afterwards the law was changed yet again and there was quite a number of suicides involving illegal immigrants from years and years before who had never bothered to register officially. As we developed techniques to seal one hole through which the illegal immigrants were pouring from China, the barons, who were reaping huge rewards for bringing these desperate people in, were using increasingly sophisticated methods to avoid detection and capture. It was a big money business. There were a lot of illegals who trekked hundreds sometimes thousands of miles to the border and simply waited until they could creep across under the cover of darkness. They would scale the border fence and find their own way into Hong Kong society. Often whole families would club together their finances to help pay the way for younger members of the family, in the hope of them finding a fresh start in the colony.

Towards the end of October 1980 we were tasked to consider techniques for use against the high-speed launches that were bringing the illegals in about twenty at a time. These boats were capable of doing forty or fifty knots and were easily outrunning any police or Navy patrol vessels. Our aircraft were hurriedly fitted with an extremely powerful searchlight known as Nite Sun. That was almost exactly what it was; this lamp could turn darkness into broad daylight. The Nite Sun had a strength of about thirty-five million candlepower and could project a beam a couple of miles and illuminate an area the size of a football pitch. But it was very difficult to fly with because the beam itself was like a huge rod or pole sticking out from the aircraft which gave us all sorts of crazy sensations, often playing havoc with our sense of balance.

We quickly realised that the best way to use it for our operations was for the aircraft to be flown from the co-pilot's left-hand seat and for the searchlight to be operated from the right-hand seat, or exceptionally

by the crewman in the cabin below. The first few operations were incredibly exciting. They involved accurate
communication and split-second timing.

We had patrols of Gurkha soldiers and marine policemen as well as our own Royal Navy and there was
obviously some pretty good intelligence coming across
from the other side. For a little while we used an infrared
beam and with the aid of special goggles we could pick
out our targets without them being aware they had been
detected. They couldn't see the beam of light nor could
they hear our rotors above the din of their own powerful
outboard motors.

We did a few practices chasing Navy speedboats and
very soon were ready to try and capture the real thing.
The plan was to follow them and then call in waiting
speedboats to wherever we thought they were going to
try to land. Early operations seemed to be quite successful
but the evening that will always stick in my mind was that
of 10 November 1981.

We were given rough vectors to a boat that was running
in across Castle Peak Bay. By this time the operation was
fairly slick and we'd had a reasonable amount of success
in recent months. We quickly picked up the boat and as
it closed in on the beach we attempted to head it off by
shining the beam directly at the coxswain. The crewman
counted a total of twenty-two people on board. They were
working very hard to avoid the beam by turning the boat
incredibly tightly; it seemed at times it was close to going
over. But we never lost them for more than a few seconds.
Eventually the boat ran aground in a small harbour next
to a tiny fishing village.

We had anticipated that this was to be their destination
and had already called for a Land Rover patrol to be

waiting on the beach for them. The boat hit the shale beach and kept on going for about thirty or forty yards, such was the speed it had been doing. By now there were only two people on board and they scrambled off the boat and into the arms of the waiting policemen.

We soon found out what had happened to the twenty others who had been on the boat because the squadron spent the next couple of days fishing out the bits the sharks had rejected from the water. The two people who were captured with the boat ended up in court and were prosecuted for not showing their navigation lights at night. They got off with a modest fine having just committed mass murder. Those terrified Chinese illegals had been callously thrown off the boat so that those who were operating a very lucrative people smuggling operation would not be caught. Up until then this had been a very exciting operation for me but I never flew a mission against the boats again – I simply did not want that on my conscience again and I made those feelings very clear to the powers that be.

It wasn't unusual to find bodies in the water and many of them were quite obviously Chinese who, with nothing more than a sealed earthenware pot to keep them afloat, had tried to make the sea crossing from mainland China to one of the Hong Kong Islands. I dare say one or two probably made it but there must have been hundreds, possibly thousands who vanished forever. A few popped up on the surface of the ocean and were nothing more than pieces of meat and a possible hazard to shipping.

On one particular day we saw a body in the water. It was a young male – we could almost always tell the difference because females float face up whereas men tend to float face down. If anyone has ever wondered why people are often discovered some days after they vanish at sea it is because shortly after a person has drowned they sink below the surface for two or three days. Then the gases in the body build up so that the corpse floats to the surface again where it is generally washed up or, a couple of days later, sinks to the bottom forever.

On this particular day the water was quite choppy and the person floating in the water seemed to be still swimming among the waves. If we had known then that he was dead we would have simply flown on. There was little point in endeavouring to fish a dead body out of the sea. No one in Hong Kong wanted another corpse. The hospitals wouldn't take them and the police mortuaries didn't want to know. There would be a mountain of paperwork and the inevitable outcome at the compulsory inquest would be death by drowning, identity unknown.

Our particular body hadn't been dead long but he was well and truly dead. The Hong Kong police used to get a bounty for handing over illegal immigrants. This was of course some form of inducement for them not to accept bribes from the immigrants themselves. Anyway, we spotted a police patrol vessel in the bay and called them up on the radio to tell them that we had a very seriously injured illegal on board and would they take him. We duly winched him down onto the aft deck of the patrol vessel. As soon as the body touched the deck we were up and away.

As we did a wide arc around the vessel to carry on about our business we watched as a couple of boatmen rolled the body off the stern of the boat and back into the water and then reversed over it cutting the corpse to shreds with the propellers. It was the most sensible thing to do and cut out all the inevitable bureaucracy that comes with a dead body. The boy's family would never know his fate and may still speak with pride about the son they believe made it to the land of great riches.

One of the tasks in which we were regularly involved was called 'fire bucket'. This exercise was carried out using a large fibreglass bucket suspended beneath the aircraft on a wire harness. In the height of the summer brush fires were commonplace and it was our job to help the fire service to put them out. At the base of the bucket were hydraulically operated doors which swung open to dump three hundred gallons of water within a couple of seconds. It was great fun. This was a team effort with beaters working on the ground and fire engines if they could get close enough to the blaze. We picked up our water from wherever we could; the sea, the odd lake or river and even the occasional private swimming pool.

In the late summer of 1980 and again during the early spring of 1981 we worked with particular fervour. On one occasion there were three squadron helicopters in a split second aerial ballet working desperately to put out an inferno which was within a few hundred yards of the block of flats in which most of us lived. Our families were all hanging out on the balconies applauding the good water drops and giving a big thumbs down for the misses. It was a mixture of fun and fear. The excitement of halting the fire's progress was combined with the realisation that if we didn't get it right our homes would be going up in flames as well.

Life was often a curious concoction of work and play. It was on the 31 of March 1981, I flew out to the maximum range of the aircraft to meet the USS *Beallau Wood*, an American aircraft carrier, about ninety miles out in the South China Sea. We carried out a few circuits, took some photos and landed on her deck in time for tea. The three of us would be spending the evening on board and would sail into Hong Kong Harbour with her.

All US ships are 'dry' in that no alcohol is ever allowed on board. Still, one night off the booze in two years was not going to do me any harm. After we'd shut down the helicopter and ensured that all of the shackles were secured, I asked the American crew chief if it was all right for me to have a smoke. He replied, 'Well, strictly speaking no, Sir, but follow me.' He led me through a maze of gantries, alleyways, bulkheads and deckheads until we eventually reached a tiny lavatory deep in the bowels of the ship.

He said that he would guard the door while I enjoyed my smoke. If I'd realised how much trouble having a simple puff on a cigarette was going to cause I would not have bothered. However, when I reached inside my breast pocket and took out my slightly crushed crush-proof packet of Benson and Hedges and put a king size filter tip to my lips, the crew chief gave out a gasp of realisation. He called through the lavatory door to me, 'Hell, Sir, I though you wanted to smoke a joint; ordinary cigarettes are OK anywhere on board!'

Work aside, the social life we enjoyed in the colony was fun with a capital F. I think one of the things I learned in the military and one of the things that people quite rightly say is that there is a huge divide between seeing a place as a holiday destination and actually living there. Hong Kong was no exception. I'd heard so many stories about the world of Suzie Wong and most were unfounded. From the days of the American Navy enjoying its furlough there to the early eighties it had cleaned up its act.

The no-go areas of Wan Chai no longer existed. We

used to enjoy a little game called a Wan Chai walkabout based on the philosophy of safety in numbers. A notice would go up on the squadron board to say that such a jaunt was to start on a Friday at 8p.m. and no one could say for certain when it was going to finish. Sometimes it lasted for four hours and sometimes for four days. I have enjoyed both sorts.

A Wan Chai walkabout was basically a pub crawl. One particularly memorable one started off with an overloaded taxi-full of seven or eight of us. But within a short time there must have been fifty or sixty servicemen and the odd tourist who joined us for the ride. The military were from all services – Army, Navy, RAF and HK Police. I still treasure a photograph of all of us at a topless bar in Wan Chai. Such was the change from the US Fifth Fleet. We walked into the bar and when the girls spotted forty or fifty red-blooded males they put all their clothes on and refused to serve us a drink. We were noisy but we didn't intend any harm. Yet the girls put their tops on and closed the bar.

It was like throwing down the gauntlet. To a man we stripped until we were stark-bollock naked and declared we would stay that way until we were served a drink. They were supposed to be topless and so we remained topless and bottomless too until they opened the bar and carried on business as normal. It was fun and I can still laugh at our behaviour. Eventually the police arrived at the scene but there was nothing they could do. We were the all-feared military and one or two quite senior officers were in our company. In the end we all got dressed again and left. Even that was amusing. Certainly the shirt I put on was too big and the trousers too short. No one cared, we all jumped in taxis and went home so it didn't really matter.

178

For a Governor's reception I was required to wear full dress uniform. It is the best Royal Air Force uniform there is, light beige in colour with the badges of rank worn on stiff shoulder boards. It costs hundreds and hundreds and certainly made me feel the business. And yet I suppose it was about three or four hours after sipping the first cocktail at this reception that I had gone off the top board of the pool at the United Services Club straight into the deep end still wearing full dress uniform and clutching my ceremonial sword. The uniform was a write off and the sword cost a week's wages to repair but it didn't seem to matter.

It must have been almost ten years after I left Hong Kong that I was still unwrapping pristine shirts made out there to wear for the very first time. You could go to Supply Squadron to be issued with an extra uniform shirt for about £5 or you could go to downtown Kowloon and buy three uniform shirts made to measure for the same price. A three-piece pinstripe suit made to measure in three and a half hours was by no means exceptional. Once again, it was part of Hong Kong life.

All the service families out there had a part-time amah or housemaid. She was either Filipino or Chinese. The Chinese tended to be more expensive and the Filipinos came cheaper in every way. Our first housemaid was called Ah Q. She had very strict rules which simply could not be broken. She would go into the soiled linen box, take out my clothes to wash, dry and iron them, then she would take Michael's clothes, soiled nappies and all to wash, dry and iron. And only if there was enough time left would she do anything about washing Sheila's dirty linen. There was no doubt about the supremacy of the master of the house and the strict order of batting: it was the man of the house, his children followed by the women.

She was constantly working around the house, dusting and polishing but she would never work in the same room as me. Sometimes, just for fun, I would follow her around. For instance, she would be dusting in the main living room and I'd walk in and sit down. Immediately she would pick up her dusters and polish – even halfway through polishing a table she would collect her things to go and work elsewhere in the house. So I would follow her, perhaps to a bedroom where she would be making up a bed. She would stop as soon as I entered the room to go and work somewhere else.

Sheila would issue her with orders of work for the day and she may or may not have carried them out, but whatever I said was law. Sometimes, particularly on a Friday night after a heavy session in the bar I would get home with two or three pals and demand bacon sandwiches and they would be served up by our amah without a hint of complaint. Quite simply the master's word was law.

Hong Kong was truly a fabulous place to be in. As officers in the Royal Air Force we were fairly high up on the social ladder. We were given automatic membership to many of the top clubs where mere mortals would probably have to wait several years and pay thousands of pounds membership fee. For instance, the Royal Hong Kong Yacht Club had a waiting list longer than your arm and yet I became a member within days of arriving on 28 Squadron.

My wife, Sheila, has always said she hated our time in Hong Kong but in the same breath admits she never ironed a shirt or washed a baby's nappy during the whole time we were there. That sort of drudgery was left to the servants. There was never a shortage of parties to go to and the booze ran freely.

It wasn't unusual for me to go out for a quick beer with a couple of pals and come back four days later. I remember one night driving home from a bar with the deputy squadron commander I shall only refer to as Mike. We were both so pissed that we were trying to drive the car between us. Needless to say we were all over the road causing all manner of mayhem when eventually a police car overtook us and forced us into the side of the road. We were giggling like a pair of schoolgirls and when the Chinese policeman walked over to open the driver's door Mike fell out into the road. The policeman recognised Mike and without saying another word he lifted him back behind the steering wheel, closed the door and returned to his patrol car to drive off. Such was the power of the military.

It was a delight to be welcomed in all the in places in town. We regularly lunched at Gaddies, the top-class restaurant attached to the world famous Peninsula Hotel. A cocktail before a show in the Bottom's Up Bar just off Nathan Road and made world famous in the James Bond movies was a favourite haunt. Visitors to Hong Kong were invariably taken to the Red Lips Bar or the old American Restaurant in Hankow Road. These places were local watering holes to us and it felt good to be that privileged, if only for a couple of years. During those two years we lived life to the full, both on and off duty. Before going out to Hong Kong we were given an enormous allowance to buy the tropical uniforms although this allowance would hardly have met the costs of a London tailor, but in the old back streets of Kowloon much could be done for little.

And in any case most of my allowance had already been spent on a new car – to hell with my uniform.

The record for me was to have a summer linen suit made within two hours, including three fittings. The tailors knew precisely how to deal with us. Before a word was exchanged an ice-cool bottle of San Miguel beer would be thrust into your hand and within the few hours that it took to make a suit many of us would have polished off the best part of a crate of beer.

A guy that I used to deal with during my time in Honkers was a chap called Tony Ko. This, you understand, had absolutely nothing to do with my Air Force duties. Anyhow, Tony dealt in precious gemstones and I soon spotted a little niche in the market for me to make a few bob. On one occasion we'd agreed a transaction which was no more than a couple of dollars over HK$20,000. Tony had been plying me with beer for an hour or so, and I wrote out a cheque and rounded it down to HK$20,000. He was absolutely enraged. We had argued, negotiated, bartered and finally reached the figure of HK$20,004. By rounding that figure down by just HK$4 it was as though I had delivered the worst insult to him. It was months before he forgave me and agreed to deal with me again.

I loved Hong Kong and absolutely adored my time there. I loved the vibrance, the chaos and most of all the pace of life. There were never enough hours in the day and I think the people around me could probably see that I was going balls out towards a brick wall in my efforts to live life to the full. There was no way that my body could keep up with that pace. If I wasn't flying then more than likely I was drinking or dealing in my own little private enterprises. There wasn't enough time to sleep, there was just so much going on and I wanted to take part. I'm certain that I never allowed my professional skills to become affected by my exuberant lifestyle. Equally, I think with the benefit of hindsight I can see that I probably became very selfish in the way that lots of things had to be done.

My own little enterprises on the Hong Kong market were in general a success and perhaps my confidence could have been read as sheer arrogance. I worked in my own way in both my private and Air Force dealings. There were two ways to do things; my way and the wrong way. What an arrogant prat I must have been. When things didn't go the way the boss wanted I was inevitably brought to task. There were horrendous bollockings, in fact most of the time.

I didn't seem to get on at all well with my boss. We had been junior officers together at Odiham and we'd got into one or two scrapes together. He seemed to hold that against me. He was now a squadron commander and almost resented the fact that I had shared in his previous life when he'd been a mere mortal. I think I went through the same phase when I was promoted to squadron leader much later in my career so I don't altogether hold it against him.

Life then seemed too short to try to be anyone other than yourself. I liked having fun and I can honestly say I am still having fun and intend to carry on doing so. I might look ten years older than I am but there is not too much that I regret.

There was always an arrival prank of some sort played on some unsuspecting young officer fresh to the squadron. When Pete Churchill arrived he was ceremoniously shown to his office because he was to be the air cadet liaison officer. He looked a bit surprised, the office we had designated for him was on the small side and had no windows. He put up with it for over a week and had even ordered himself a desk from Supply Squadron; that was until someone let on to him that in fact he was working from the squadron's broom cupboard and the cleaning staff had asked when could they have it back. I think his reaction to the silly tricks department was fairly well contained although he raised certain questions about our individual parentage!

Being in Hong Kong it was hard to avoid the smell of money and the lure of big business. One or two of us dabbled on the stock market with varying degrees of success. For a brief period I was totally under its spell and every spare second of my time was spent scouring the financial papers ready to make that one pitch that would turn me into an overnight millionaire. I'm happy – and relieved – to say that I got out by the skin of my teeth. I'd enjoyed several months of good fortune and my salary was close to a pittance compared to what I was turning out from the stock market. I was easily trebling the £15,000 a year I earned from the Royal Air Force.

Then the run of bad luck started. My overdraft back in the UK was bringing tears to the bank manager's eyes and I think he was very close to pulling the rug from under me. He wrote me a letter which, by the time it arrived, gave me just about a week to sort things out. I did the only thing I could think of and that was to send him a cheque for the full amount. The only problem was that the cheque was written from the account that was already so desperately overdrawn. I was relying on the bank manager's sense of humour to give me those few extra hours' stay of execution that I needed. It worked. He telephoned me saying 'OK you sod. Another week, absolute tops and that's it.' With only days to spare I turned some stock in a very risky Australian mining operation but it paid off the overdraft, gave me a handsome profit and I never touched the Hong Kong stock market again.

Approaching the end of my two-year tour the postings man came out to visit and explained that I would be going to Shawbury in Shropshire to teach basic helicopter flying. The very thought turned my stomach. I told him that I was going to be a guinea pig and was required to fly the RAF's latest and most advanced fighter bomber, the Tornado. It was all part of an experiment to see if experienced helicopter pilots would be able to adapt to the vastly different and extremely demanding pressures of the fast jet cockpit. In fact, I had just made the whole thing up, but the last thing I wanted to do while still breathing was to teach and anyway I fancied a bit of a change.

When I got my posting to the fast jet crossover it was to start at the end of April. I was over the moon, especially as all of my colleagues had said that not only did I not stand a snowflake in hell's chance of being posted to Tornados, but even if I was I wouldn't pass the course. The only dampener to my new challenge was that the posting clashed horribly with the birth of our baby daughter, Eleanor. At the time, Sheila was heavily pregnant with our second child who was due to be born at the beginning of May 1982.

The squadron commander refused to lift a hand to try to change my posting date, explaining how it was all too difficult. However, a couple of phone calls later to some friends in high places back at the Ministry of Defence and my posting was delayed by a couple of months. Eleanor was born on 5 May in Hong Kong. We moved back to the UK six weeks later and I enjoyed a month's leave with my family before embarking on yet another new and exciting adventure.

7

Back in the Fast Lane

After six weeks' glorious summer leave I pitched up at RAF Leeming in North Yorkshire during the first week of August 1982 to start my fast jet crossover training. Initially, it was back to the classroom in a large Edwardian-type building with thirty or forty postwar desks and a huge blackboard and overhead projector at the front.

I'd always been extremely averse to classrooms of any sort but there was no chance of me sitting at the back and dozing off here, because the staff to pupil ratio was one to one – I was the only person on the course! In the event the ground school was quite painless. I passed the requisite exams and went across to the other side of the hangar to join the school of refresher flying.

There were four Jet Provost aircraft, half a dozen or so instructors and two pupils – myself and Phil Keating, an old pal from helicopter days who'd obviously spun a similar yarn to me. In fact we both ended up on the same Tornado squadron together but after a couple of years he went back to helicopters.

My first instructor was an old pal from basic flying training days, Ian Ferguson. Ian had flown the Phantom Supersonic Fighter for a couple of tours before having a

brain transplant to become a flying instructor. I heard that
Ian actually suffered a massive heart attack some years
later and will never fly again. I'm just glad he survived
– he is a good man.

Training on the Jet Provost took almost exactly a month
during which time I relearned the basic skills of flying a
fixed-wing aircraft. The course was supposed to last about
thirty-five hours but I managed to complete most of the
tasks in fairly quick time and was released with four or
five hours to spare. I certainly needed those when it came
to flying the Hawk at RAF Valley later.

The Jet Provost could fly at about 300 knots downhill
with the wind but a speed of 240 knots was much more
usual. I had been used to flying the Wessex for so many
years now at about half that speed but only fifty feet or
so above the ground. Navigation of the Jet Provost at
250 feet was an absolute doddle by comparison. It may
sound conceited, but the truth is I regularly ended up
teaching my own instructors how to navigate the aircraft
at low level.

My last trip in the Jet Provost was 17 September 1982
and it was almost the last day of my life. I was to fly a close
formation detail with Squadron Leader Pete Rayment.
Paul McDonald was flying the lead aircraft. We took
off from runway one-eight at Leeming on a particularly
misty afternoon. Within seconds of leaving the ground I
became completely befuddled as to which way was up and
I think for an instant I had no idea how to control the
aeroplane. I started thrashing wildly at the controls. We
skidded underneath the other aircraft, it could only have
been 100 feet or so above the ground and to pull away at
that level would have meant impact with our leader.

Squadron Leader Rayment screamed 'For fuck's sake'

then wrestled control from me and eased the aircraft into the clear blue sky above the layer of mist. He eased us gently back into close formation and coolly asked if I would like to try that one again, adding would I try not to kill him as his wife was preparing his favourite roast beef for dinner that evening.

The rest of the sortie progressed reasonably well and I was soon back into the swing of flying one aircraft just a few feet from another. I was expecting and fully deserved an absolute bollocking during the subsequent debrief but Squadron Leader Rayment was most apologetic. He had assumed that this was to be another well-flown sortie by me. The course had gone very well up until then, surely close formation flying would present no real problems at all. However, I hadn't flown close formation in a fixed-wing aircraft for almost ten years. He reminded us both that you must never assume someone's proficiency but always, always check first before it is too late.

My six weeks at Leeming drew to a close and I moved on to RAF Valley on the island of Anglesey, North Wales. I had flown the Gnat at Valley during the summer of 1975 so the station and all the pubs within a radius of five miles were still quite familiar to me. It was back to school again with another two weeks in the classroom with only myself and the instructor.

The distinct advantage for me was that there was a Hawk simulator at Valley and I spent every spare minute that I could either learning checks or trying to come to grips with this pocket rocket. Within months, the Hawk had become a close friend to me. It is a beautiful aeroplane to fly. The controls have a superb harmony, the view from the cockpit is magnificent and performance wise it compares easily with many modern-day fighters.

But those early days back in the world of the fast jet were absolutely terrifying. I felt about as sharp as a beachball with a slow puncture. I was about twelve years older than most of the students of RAF Valley and because technically mine was a refresher course I was expected to be able to complete my training within a fraction of the time it was going to take them.

I've often said since that if I had realised just how hard conversion to fast jets was going to be then I would never have done it. Many evenings I was in bed by 8 o'clock totally knackered from one, two and sometimes three sorties flown during that day. My brain hurt and it felt like every muscle in my body wanted to scream from the sheer physical and mental effort that was being drawn from me.

The scheme of assessing a pilot's progress during training had changed dramatically from the cloak and dagger days of my basic training. Now, any time you wanted to see your training folder or view the instructor's assessments you just went to the filing cabinet and pulled out your personal file. It was so bloody frustrating to see my performance as low average and below average. Some trips were rated as poor. But I just could not have given one more ounce of effort. Here I was scraping along at the bottom of the barrel, when a few months earlier I had been rated as an exceptional pilot.

It took nearly three months instead of the expected two for me to finally make the grade. Approaching Christmas and the end of the course I eventually passed out on 2 December 1982 with a low average assessment but an above average potential. I didn't know whether to laugh or cry.

My course at RAF Chivenor in north Devon wasn't

due to start until mid-January. However, I was back in the cockpit within days of leaving Valley. I would dream up any excuse I could find to get airborne at every opportunity. My determination paid off in the end. I had already vowed to work until I dropped at Chivenor. My course there started with about a dozen students and it was a relief to share a classroom with others and their problems, even if I was the grandad of them all.

I was the course leader which as much as anything involved taking care of fellow pupils' domestic problems. I really enjoyed it. By the time the course finished half the intake had fallen by the wayside. They had been chopped from fast jets to become anything from secretarial officers to navigators.

Most of the instructors at Chivenor were guys that I had gone through basic training with years before. I found I had much more in common with them than with my fellow students. My performance on the aeroplane was improving almost daily. My assessments by now were average to high average with the occasional above average thrown in for good measure. What's more, I even felt that there were odd occasions when I was actually enjoying my flying again. I was prepared to do anything to get onto the Tornado. My whole life revolved around that single ambition. Every other night I used to run from home right around the airfield, sometimes twice. It was sheer hard slog all the way but it still didn't stop me enjoying a few beers at Friday night's happy hour.

Chivenor was the place where you learned to be a warrior. Flying an aeroplane at low level or in close formation or navigating with pinpoint accuracy has to come as naturally as negotiating your way down a busy street. By now, I was required to do precisely what the

191

taxpayer's money paid for – to use the aircraft as a
weapons platform. I don't think I have ever considered
myself a warrior. Professional killers, after all, is what we
in the military professions are supposed to be. I would
certainly accept being called a professional marksman and
put myself and my contemporaries on a par with a doctor,
lawyer or a highly skilled engineer. But until I actually took
life as a member of Her Majesty's Forces, I had never really
sat down and thought about what it meant.

Chivenor for me was the most forgiving spring of
1983 which led on to a beautiful summer. Much of the
flying was solo; there would be one sortie flown with an
instructor and then three or four to consolidate what you
had learned. Every day was just full of excitement, there
was always something new. The course was beautifully
designed. Every time you felt remotely capable of yet
another skill you went on to learn something new again.
You never had time to consolidate. By the end of the
training, even the straight-through students had cost the
taxpayer around £5 million. With that sort of money
being spent no one was going to accept responsibility for
wasting a single second.

By the end of the course I think most of us felt a sort
of superiority that there were none better. We had been
honed to perfection, tuned to the perfect pitch. There was
a tremendous feeling of well-being and I suppose in many
ways our social high jinks were explainable. We were
almost caged animals and if ever we were going to be
called into battle as fighter pilots then our training had
prepared us magnificently. If you are going to survive you
have to be totally confident, absolutely ruthless, supremely
capable. Your reactions have to be split second, your
co-ordination has to exceed anything required of a top

trapeze artist performing the most dare-devil stunts. Only the best will do and when you reach that standard the next target is to surpass it. With a couple of beers on top of all of this, who could fail to understand and excuse the odd exuberant outburst?

When you are running into a bomber target using a three-kilogram practice bomb, which gave off a small burst of brightly coloured smoke on impact, the target spotter would give you your score within seconds. When running in we were expected to get within thirty or forty feet of the target which was a very tall order. The aiming reticle was the most rudimentary affair. Basically it was gyroscopically balanced and it projected a red circle of light onto the windscreen ahead. In the centre of the circle was a single dot of light known as the pipper. When the pipper was over the target you pressed the weapon's release button and dropped the bomb off.

All you could do with the weapon aiming reticle was programme the height above the target that you planned to fly and the expected wind speed and direction. It was a very approximate affair. During the target run the aircraft crossed the ground at the rate of 800 feet a second and we were expected to get the bombs within fifty feet of the target which, if all else worked, meant that you had to push the button to an accuracy of one sixteenth of a second otherwise you would be 800 feet out.

During the strafing attacks we had to dive at an angle of about fifteen degrees and machine gun a fifteen-foot square white sheet. If you opened fire a second too early then all of the bullets would fall short of the target. Then, if you were really unlucky, you would fly into the ground or at least just beyond the target thankfully missing death by the skin of your teeth. It was incredibly exciting and incredibly exhilarating. In many ways you really were staring death in the face and giving it a statutory two fingers.

Every so often somebody did hit the ground. If he was incredibly lucky he would bang out and report to the station commander for his bollocking. If he didn't get away with it and bought it then we'd have a few drinks on his bar book, tell his widow or his mum what a good guy he was, wait a day or so until the mess had been cleared up and then get on with our training.

In the latter days of the training everything was lumped in together to fill an hour and a half sortie. Four aircraft would launch into the sky in a tactical battle formation followed by a fifth a few minutes later. The formation would be led by a student who had probably spent days preparing to lead his mission. And after an hour and a half he would be torn to shreds by the instructional staff.

Number four in the formation would usually be an instructor who would play the dumb-arsed tail-end Charlie while witnessing every single solitary mistake of the three aircraft ahead of him. The fifth aircraft behind us would play the part of a Soviet fighter. His job was to get in among the formation and try to simulate shooting us down – as if we weren't in enough trouble.

We'd leave Chivenor flying at low level across the Bristol Channel to make a first run attack at Pembrey Range in South Wales, then on through the coal mining valleys and up to the mountains of Snowdonia. Two hundred and fifty feet was the regulation low flying height and 800 feet a second was the normal low flying speed. We were just over a quarter of a second from the ground. We were to run into two targets during the navigation part of the sortie. Each target would rarely be more than a few feet square, say for instance a plank over a small stream or a telephone box.

I was running alongside the number two aircraft in good formation, about 2,000 yards line-abreast with my leader. I had a quick look back over my right shoulder to check the other two aircraft a mile or so behind and in perfect formation. Half a second in which to relax but no, bollocks, eyes teeming as I squinted into the sun.

If he is coming at all that is where he will come from, the faintest speck growing larger all the time. 'Buster' the call for everyone to go to full power then 'counter starboard, go', the stomach-churning six-and-a-half-G turn towards our aggressor. 'Roll out heading 135' – not the direction we want to go in but we don't want to get shot down either. The aggressor flies head to head through the formation and as he passes the rear aircraft he pulls high and rolls right for another shot.

'Reverse, counter port, roll out 315 degrees'; back on track but where has he gone? Everyone's eyes are out on organ stops. Number three calls: 'visual no tally', which means he can see the rest of the formation but not the aggressor. Suddenly from behind a rocky outcrop a Hawk at 400 yards appears astern of the number three. A smug and contented call from the bandit 'Fox Two' which means he would have launched an air-to-air missile shooting number three from the sky. The whole engagement probably lasted no more than thirty or forty seconds and the formation would have been attacked between four and six times. Then we went back to base; total duration one and a half hours.

Some medical boffins came and had a look at us during our time on the course and with some alarm they noted that we could lose two or three pounds in body weight during such a sortie. It came as no surprise to us.

Air-to-air gunnery was another of those black arts. A Hawk would be sent up into the sky trailing about 400 or 500 yards of wire and behind that a white canvas streamer called the banner. Our job was to try and shoot the banner. Each aircraft was fitted with a single barrel Aden cannon mounted beneath the fuselage.

We had about eighty or ninety rounds each to play with and each belt of ammunition was painted in a different colour. So four or five aircraft would fly a racetrack pattern around the banner each taking his turn to shoot, and when the banner was delivered back to Chivenor you would scurry out there and count the number of holes etched with your particular colour. This was a skill that I never particularly mastered, suffice it to say that there were never many holes in my colour.

Air combat could also be lumped in with these mystic skills that you either had or had not. It involved going into the air in one aircraft and your instructor in another. You would climb in close formation to about 10,000 feet and then run away from each other for about a minute. After the inbound turn and confirmation of visual contact the game would be on, the object being for each to try and shoot the other down.

I am told that I was quite good at air combat but it never seemed that way from my seat in the cockpit. For most of the time after we had passed each other head on I just applied full power and kept the stick back in my stomach pulling to the maximum seven-G limit, and it appeared that all I was trying to do was vanish up my own backside.

What I really loved was the low-level navigation and

I only ever wanted to fly the Tornado because of its low-flying supremacy. My results towards the end of the course had been pretty good. My flight commander, Mike Malone, a lovely little Scotsman who now flies for Cathay Pacific, did his best to persuade me to fly single seaters. He urged me to try and get on to the Lightning or the Jaguar or Harrier. But I was having none of it. Despite the navigator in the back seat I still wanted to fly the Tornado.

On 21 April 1983 I passed my weapons training course and received the prize for the best overall student of the year and the best weaponry student. It seemed a million years from those awful weeks at Valley just months before where I had come so close to failure. Those who were left on the course and graduated with me applied for all sorts of exotic postings while they waited for their respective operational conversion units. I'd fallen into that trap once before and asked to stay at Chivenor in order to get as many spare Hawk rides as I could.

Having completed my course with flying colours it was a tremendous relief to shed all that pressure from my shoulders and my thoughts. I was back in the cockpit doing exactly the same routines and sortie profiles yet without the almost unbearable responsibility of knowing I was being assessed every second of the way. By the middle of June I was leading student sorties and enjoying every minute of it.

An exercise we flew known as Exercise Priory was to be my first experience of flying with navigators in the back seat of the Hawk. It was part of a new scheme whereby navigators were being brought to Chivenor to spend a few sorties before going on to their respective conversion units. But it seemed to me that no one had the faintest clue about what to do with them. As many of the instructors came from the intensity of the single seaters the regular instruction seemed to be that they should sit in the back, keep quiet and touch nothing.

Anyway, I flew with Pete Ritchie who was on the staff at Chivenor, an ex-Buccaneer navigator with a wealth of experience and a library full of tall stories. The exercise involved large Hawk formations trying to break through the air defence network protecting the east coast of the United Kingdom. It lasted a little over a week and we flew one or two sorties a day from our temporary base at RAF Finningley in South Yorkshire.

We took off from the base, climbed to high altitude and headed east. As soon as we got to the Dutch air space boundary we would turn around, dive to low level and run hell for leather towards the defensive radar stations in East Anglia. It was great sport. The Phantoms or Lightnings which were sent to intercept us were much faster but nowhere near as manoeuvrable as our baby jets. We could easily be compared with irritating flies buzzing around a picnic table.

On one occasion I recall running in as part of a wider formation. We were flat out which for us meant about 450 knots or 500mph. As we were so far from land we were allowed down to 100 feet above the sea. Pete spotted the first formation diving towards us. Typically they were coming straight out of the sun. As we turned and twisted I spared a thought to try and work out why Pete appeared to be able to see directly behind us. I managed to get a quick look over my shoulder and it was most amusing to see this guy kneeling on his seat and facing backwards. He'd even undone his straps to get a proper look at what was going on. We never discussed it at any great length but I felt very proud that he should put his life so very obviously in my hands. He had taken his safety net away, trusting that I would take good care of him.

Pete had always been a dyed-in-the-wool fast-jet navigator and yet the next time I saw him was when I led a detachment of Tornados to Cyprus where he was a helicopter crewman with 84 Squadron and enjoying every minute of it. I asked him how he managed to arrange a crossover from fast jets to helicopters. He just winked and smiled as he told me that I wasn't the only one with friends in high places.

It was just over a week later on 29 July 1983 that I got as close as I ever want to be to meeting my maker. I described the incident fully in my book *Pablo's War*. It could have been an omen of what was to come – I don't believe that but I do accept that fate has a funny way of playing out our lives.

The Iraqi student who so nearly brought about my death some eight years before I went to war against his countrymen could have ended the story there. It was a lovely Friday afternoon, a gin-clear summer's day. I was looking forward to a few beers at happy hour, the only fly in the ointment was that the new commander in chief had decided that no flying suits were to be worn in the bar in future. That evening was to be the last day before the new rule was imposed.

Along with a couple of pals I had scrounged as many old flying suits as I could and we had arranged these on a coat rack outside the entrance to the bar. As a final gesture of defiance we had decided that for this last Friday no one would be allowed in the bar unless they were wearing a flying suit. I almost got back to the flight line without enough time to prepare for the afternoon's sortie.

Nigel Risdale was about to take my place. I remember

standing in the operations room and the telephone rang; the caller was trying to find Wing Commander George Lee, OC operations. He was in the crew room when he took the call. A Hawk had just crashed, initially it was believed to be from our base. However, it transpired that it was from RAF Brawdy, our sister weapons training station in South Wales. Wing Commander Lee made it very clear that, unless the plane had flown from his station, it was not his responsibility, before firmly replacing the receiver on its cradle. Little did he suspect that within two hours he was to lose two of his own jets.

We took off from the westerly runway of Chivenor turning right shortly after takeoff and right again to skirt the north coast of Devon. Two aircraft were in formation, me sitting behind Pete Sheppard and Mike Phillips behind his Iraqi student. It was to be a simple two-ship formation where we would spend most of the time abreast at low level as we practised turns and reversals. If there was time at the end we would climb to a few thousand feet and carry out a tail chase. This would involve the number two aircraft flying in a cone of space about 400 yards behind his leader, keeping that position no matter what the leader does. It is a technique that was developed for aerial combat. It is quite a challenging exercise and it is also jolly good fun.

We turned south to skirt the eastern verges of Dartmoor, passing Okehampton and heading down towards Dartmoor prison which we were never allowed to overfly; on then to a westerly heading and then gently easing up to fly our planned tail chase. The sortie had gone very well so far. The Iraqi student had always retained a near-perfect position or on the odd occasion that he had missed his slot he sorted himself out very quickly.

Pete and I had taken turns to fly the aircraft and now it was my turn. We were up at a few thousand feet almost overhead the village of Hamworthy in north Devon. I carried out a few gentle turns and with encouragement from Pete I was starting to wind things up. The student was doing very well but we both decided he needed toughening up. I began to put more aggression into my manoeuvres pulling that little bit harder and adding an extra crispness to entry and exit from the turns.

Most of the time I could easily see the number two aircraft in one of my three canopy-mounted rear-view mirrors. Suddenly, during a pitch-up manoeuvre he vanished from sight. I expected him to come back into view within seconds. If you lost sight of your tail chaser for more than ten seconds then the call was 'Knock it off' which meant fly straight and level into clear air space and we will sort things out from there.

I was just about to make that call when the whole canopy ahead filled with aeroplane. For a split second I could see every rivet and blemish on the side of the fuselage. Then there was a sickening almighty bang as we collided. To this day I can still vividly recall an aircraft spinning towards the ground and yet my recall is entirely wrong. It was subsequently proved by the accident investigators that the other aircraft had burst into two main pieces on impact and was a blazing inferno within a few seconds. But, thank God, those few seconds had been long enough for Mike and his student to eject safely.

Pete took control of our aircraft, bits were falling off and rattling along the fuselage behind me. As the smoke in the cockpit began to thin I could make out that very few of the flight or engine instruments were working and the central warning panel was lit up like a Christmas tree.

No emergency that I had ever practised in the simulator had prepared me for this.

We flew back towards Chivenor and Pete, a Navy lieutenant commander on exchange duties, was using his thirty-odd years of flying experience to handle the aircraft by the seat of his pants. He made a magnificent job of it. Fortunately the radio was still working and he made a mayday call to Chivenor. Another aircraft was vectored towards us in order for the crew to carry out an external inspection to assess our condition. Malcolm Howell was flying this other aircraft and he seemed most reluctant to close in within a few hundred yards of us. Bigger and bigger bits were falling away from us all the time.

The radio frequency was now entirely ours and Pete told Malcolm that we had indications of two main wheel green lights, therefore our main landing gear was down and locked. But there was no indication at all as to the position of the nose wheel. Malcolm's voice crackled over the radio that the portion of the fuselage from the base of the windscreen forwards was missing. Pete coolly replied, 'Well, I don't suppose I am going to get a nose wheel green then.'

The noise in the cockpit was incredibly loud. We had obviously lost our pressurisation and Pete commented to me that we had to do something fairly soon because his feet were getting rather cold. In fact they were sticking out into a 200mph breeze. We then had quite a hefty discussion, there was no way Pete wanted us to attempt to land the aircraft. On touchdown, if the fuselage tipped forwards it would grind his legs away before we stopped. He wanted us both to bang out.

An ejection seat is designed to save your life but it is certainly not a comfortable ride The first few seconds of an ejection will subject your body to stresses and strains which are almost certain to break something. There is no doubt that you are going to get more bruises than the entire England rugby pack after a major international game. I just felt at that stage that I wasn't going to give up the aeroplane without a fight. I also remember talking to George Lee back at our base on the radio and him telling us that whatever we elected to do was fine by him. He just wanted us back in one piece.

But there were many things left unsaid. In a split second four feet or so had been sliced off the front of the fuselage and we didn't know if what was left of the aircraft would withstand two ejections without disintegrating around us. In a slightly subdued voice Wing Commander Lee told us that he had cleared the control tower and was there anything we wanted to say in private. It was a strange sensation and it must be brought about by the military training. There is a detachment that happens in your head. You feel emotion and fear and a desperation to be with your loved ones but another chunk of your mind which retains control drives you to get on with it and to put all those other sensations to one side.

Anyway there was nothing that I wanted to say and Pete stayed silent too. It was time to bite the bullet. We decided to level at 6,000 feet over Barnstaple Bay where Pete would bale out. I would stay with the aircraft and attempt to land it back at Chivenor. We agreed that I would close my eyes tightly as Pete counted downwards from three before ejecting. I would wait a few seconds for the debris to clear and then open my eyes to see what was left.

Three, two, one, ejecting. Eyes tightly closed. A loud bang and an enormous rush of warm air. I counted slowly and deliberately to four and then opened my eyes. I could see the rocket pack and seat immediately in front of me. My slow and deliberate count had probably lasted less than half a second. I watched with fascination as Pete roared skywards and the automatics tipped him from his seat and deployed his parachute.

However, I was still in what was left of the aircraft. It was tipping back and forth like a bucking bronco, the controls were sluggish and beginning to seize up. The engine was making a horrible clattering noise, certainly in its death throes. I pressed the transmit button called ejecting and pulled the handle.

Apparently Pete could hear me singing half a mile away. I also ran through my entire repertoire of swear words at the top of my voice before finally hitting the water. I was picked up by Geoff Roberts, an old pal from my Wessex days, and flown back to Chivenor still in one piece. It transpired that the only injury to any of the four of us was a nasty bruise on the back of Mike Phillip's head, which had happened at Barnstaple Hospital. When I went into the casualty room I was so pleased to see the others had survived that I rushed towards Mike and he fell backwards off his seat bashing the back of his head on the floor. Mike thought I was about to take a swipe at him, blaming him for nearly killing us all. It was quite the opposite; I was simply overjoyed to see him alive.

After a couple of X-rays I was back at Chivenor medical centre for a night under observation. Or so they thought. I had other plans and so did Pete Sheppard. With split-second timing and a brief plan, Pete went out of the ward window as I slipped out through the lavatory window. We had a couple of nurses guarding the main exit as I think they knew what was on our mind. We regrouped in the officer's mess bar by 7p.m. well into the evening's happy hour and still wearing the soggy flying suits we had ejected in.

First thing on Monday morning we were flown to RAF Wroughton for a complete medical check-up. The doctors said that we should rest for at least a month. Pete Sheppard was put into a surgical collar but I joked with him that it had more to do with his imminent retirement and schemes to apply for a disability pension rather than a few pains in his neck. I was back flying within three days none the worse for my experience.

8

The Tornado Days
on XV and 16 Squadrons

I can honestly say that my experiences as a pilot on a Royal Air Force fighter bomber squadron were both the best and the very worst days of my life. I was there; there was nowhere else to go, I was a king among kings and a god among gods. All those years of planning and desire and ambition were finally realised and in the early days most definitely it was all that I had dreamed of.

As a teenager standing on the apron at RAF Leuchars and listening to every single syllable uttered by Pilot Officer Morgan as he described the Lightning fighter, my only desire was to be up there with the best one day. I wanted to meet Officer Morgan again to tell him: 'Once, I remember worshipping you as one of the gods. Now, here I am, standing shoulder to shoulder with you and I am one of those gods.'

It's easy to be dismissive when you have arrived and to assure others that you are nothing special and just 'doing your job'. But it was never true. I felt special because I was. And it is not mere arrogance, it is a statement of fact.

Each one of us on this earth exists despite odds of millions to one against, a result of that one relationship and that one month and that one egg and one sperm. Then

207

years later through life finally you can look around like a mountaineer standing on the top of the world, Mount Everest, where else is there to go?

For the seven years that I was based at RAF Laarbruch in West Germany I was that mountaineer standing at the peak of my profession. I think that there was a brief reflection to my helicopter days when often I would be introduced to people socially and when they inquired as to precisely what I did and I answered that I was a helicopter pilot then, whether or not it was there, I always sensed a slight disappointment in their reactions. They were happy enough to meet a Royal Air Force pilot but if they wanted to advance up the military social scale then I would be rapidly passed over.

In the old black and white Bogart movies everyone looked towards the door when the leggy blonde entered the room. I wasn't a helicopter pilot anymore, I was the leggy blonde. Throughout my RAF career there had always been a slight aching in my stomach that I had still not arrived at where I really wanted to be – I was still second best and hungry for the chance to become a fighter pilot. When I look back from the comfortable seat of a modern-day airliner, I am just so desperately proud in the sure knowledge that I have done it all. In terms of a flying career, I would not swap a single second with anyone.

There was a delay between completing my weapons training at RAF Chivenor and the start of my conversion training onto the Tornado at RAF Cottesmore in Rutland. I finished the weapons course in the third week of April 1983 but I wasn't due to start on Tornados until November – almost seven months away. In the mid-seventies when I had completed my training on the Folland Gnat I had wasted the few months between then and weapons training and subsequently failed the course to end up being chopped from the Hawker Hunter. By the skin of my teeth I was re-rolled onto helicopters. This time there were to be no mistakes and only minimum risks. Throughout the entire time between flying Hawks and then the Tornado I worked like fury to guarantee that I would stay at my peak as a Top Gun.

Even now I still have no doubt that I was at my sharpest as a fighter pilot on 21 April 1983. That was the day I flew my final sortie in weapons training back at RAF Chivenor. And yet, even then, there were other guys who were better than me – my instructors Steve Riley, Mike Phillips, Dick Cole and Adam Stoaling. It seemed to me that Adam Stoaling could control a massive formation of fighter aircraft in the most calm and calculated manner and also to perfection while completing *The Times* crossword inside forty seconds at the same time. Steve Riley was the sort of guy who, in aerial combat, found odds of five to one against rather mundane. He could go up against any three of the best combat pilots in the Air Force and 'kill 'em with film' which is to confirm, in the comfort of the debriefing cinema, that had his aircraft been armed with bullets rather than celluloid he would have shot them to shreds before they were even aware he had been there.

After a period of ground school that carried me through the autumn of 1983, I flew my first ever Tornado sortie on 2 November 1983. A misty shroud hung over the old turf and sandy plough-covered land around Cottesmore. The birds were just beginning to sing and the light was barely glinting on the horizon in the eastern sky. It was magnificent. First light, the time when all warriors should go to war; the dawning of a new day.

I'd had some introduction to what I should expect from the Tornado because I had already flown six sorties in the Tornado simulator which is an incredibly real sensation. But, as I was about to find out, it was absolutely nothing like the real thing.

My instructor, Uli Glockner, a German Naval officer, was full of fun and anxious to swap jokes and banter about the Second World War. We enjoyed breakfast together in the twenty-four-hour restaurant in the officers' mess and then caught the crew coach to our aircraft waiting on the pan. The serial number of the Tornado trainer was G4316 indicating that she belonged to the Luftwaffe. The allocation of aircraft at Cottesmore was a strict percentage of Tornados provided to each nation involved – Britain, Germany and Italy. The differences between each nation's aircraft were very subtle and amounted to little more than a different radio or an instrument placed in a slightly different position.

By the time I flew my very last Tornado sortie in May of 1991 I could get the beast airborne from a standing start within three minutes. But that first day it was going to be more like an hour and a half before we would taxi forward under our own power. This fourteen-tonne monster over which I was supposed to have absolute control was entirely in control of me. I could sense the aeroplane gloating at my inadequacy.

So many people tell me that aircraft are just so much metal, rubber and fuel. But it is just not true. Each one of them has a soul and there is no doubt that each one possesses the spirit of a woman. The fire, the commitment and the desire of every man to control and possess that aircraft is all consuming. If you can show that you are the master then a tender caress will draw out your every desire. But if there is one minuscule weakness in your skills then she will eat you alive, drawing you in and then spitting you out in pieces.

You go into the engineering hut and sign for the aircraft on an RAF form 700. Little has changed in the layout since 1914. After reading through all the recent servicing, the ADDs – acceptable deferred defects – the flight limitation's log and then finally adding a signature the aircraft belongs to me; all £33 million of it in the true military sense – I've signed for it so it's mine.

The initial checks to start the engines of a front-line fighter are known as the 'left to rights'. You progress around the cockpit from well behind the left shoulder to well behind the right shoulder. The vital knobs and tits are within easy eye-shot – dead ahead on the forward panel. But the living space aboard one of Her Majesty's fighters is of necessity tiny; every nook and cranny is utilised to the full.

You don't so much start a Tornado as awaken it. All of the systems are waiting like a dragon in her lair to be disturbed and finally unleashed. As a pilot it was merely my job to awaken that slumbering creature and fit its harness ready for action. Gradually the systems whine into action and from a dormant and silent hulk there are stirrings of ever-increasing intensity. The aircraft creaks and groans into life as she awakens and begins to snort and stamp like a hungry lioness.

A simple switch moved to the right; green light on and the first engine is alight. Moments later from a touch of the same switch the second engine is stirring. Two Rolls-Royce RB 199s humming in perfect harmony. At tickover you could hold a conversation within fifty yards of the aircraft. At full throttle the earth moves and nobody gets a word in.

Canopy down, chocks away. A simple wave to the mortal ground crew, after all, I am a god. A touch of power and then a dab on the brakes, the aircraft eases forward and bows with a grandiose gesture towards its marshaller who supervised our start up. Then, a clipped transmission to the tower: 'Alpha one-nine taxi' and a sexy reply: 'Alpha one nine clear taxi to runway two seven. QNH one zero one seven.' The female controller cleared me to the westerly runway and the setting for my altimeter is a few millibars above normal. As I listened to the WRAF officer at the other end of the radio I wondered, just for that fleeting second, what she looked like and how she performed in bed. I am after all a god. There is no doubt about the supreme arrogance of a fighter pilot; you are a god because you have to be.

The taxi checks and the pre-takeoff checks are delivered 'challenge and response'. My instructor and navigator for the trip, Uli, reads from a checklist the vital actions before we can get safely airborne. He calls out 'flaps' and I respond 'to take off'. Several more checks and then there can be no more excuses.

'Alpha one nine ready for departure', and the female voice responds 'Alpha one nine clear takeoff, surface wind two-four-zero ten knots'. There is a nervous expectancy; you want to go but you don't. Here is terra firma and it is safe and cossetting. So far, the aeroplane has done precisely what you want it to but in a few seconds' time one Panavia Tornado is going to be in its element and within two minutes you could be over 30,000 feet away from your own. It is the awareness that, as the throttle levers go forward, the aeroplane is more in control of itself than you are, so you stand on the brakes, right hand holding the joystick control column so tightly that your knuckles seem to be bursting out through the white cape leather gloves.

Your left hand is balanced between both throttles, left hand forward to the first detent and this is the stage when the aircraft appears to have a mind of its own. It bucks and whips, desperate to get airborne. But your feet are held in clay, clinging on to the pedal-mounted foot brakes. An instantaneous check of the engine instruments shows that everything is perfectly normal and there are no more excuses. You push the throttle through the gate and into reheat. In an instant you have just more than doubled the thrust from the engines.

Brakes off and 'oh fuck' – and I can tell you now, that is exactly what it is like. The numbers on the airspeed indicator go out of control racing forwards as you out-accelerate the fastest sports car ever built. The lightest touch on the control column and the windscreen is suddenly full of sky. The urgent necessity to raise the undercarriage before it is torn off in the slipstream just takes over. There is no time to think before the flaps need to be raised. The whole exercise becomes frantic. You burst through this gossamer skin that has so far tried to tie you to the earth. But as the fear is torn away you glide into perfect harmony with the machine you had feared was ready to run away with you.

That very first Tornado flight will be etched on my memory forever. There was the feeling of being at a local dance and asking someone you have never seen before to join you on the dance floor only to realise that if your name was Fred Astaire then you are partnering Ginger Rogers. My conversion to being competent to fly the

Tornado was completed by the end of January. Much of the training was flown with instructors although many of them had relatively few hours on the Tornado because it was such a new aeroplane.

The 'solo flights' were flown with an ex-Phantom navigator from the Luftwaffe, Peter Stutz. Peter and I became firm friends, however, we were both nations and classes apart. He was German aristocracy through and through while I was some oik from Birmingham. My salary was my life blood, his was pocket money. Short of a duelling scar on his cheek, Peter was the archetypal German nobleman. That was until one trip in early January by which time I had decided he was totally lacking in any sense of humour. But on that trip we where flying along when Peter suddenly called out 'Hey, Pablo, you are British and I am German, and the aeroplane we are flying belongs to the Italian Air Force, where are we going to drop the bombs?'

I often wonder what Peter is doing now because since those early days we lost touch as I moved on with my young family and he moved on with his – I in my battered old Ford saloon car and he in his air-conditioned Mercedes. We never decided where we would drop that bomb.

RAF Cottesmore is a military flying station like no other. Its official title is the TTTE – the Tri-National Tornado Training Establishment. However, all and sundry knew it as Thomas The Tank Engine. The station was run by the three nations involved – Germany, Italy and the United Kingdom. Each nation paid a percentage of the cost into a pot. While the station commander was always an RAF group captain, the chief flying instructor for example would rotate through the three nations.

Cottesmore is quite simply a money magnet and it seems that each of the nations is in direct competition with each other to throw as much loot into the place as they can. All officers' messes are beautifully laid out but Cottesmore had that extra touch – exceptional sporting facilities, and every blade of grass around the station neatly manicured. It was a nice place to be because you got to learn so much about the culture of the other nations. For instance, the Germans would always greet each other very formally: 'Good morning, Herr Stutz; Good morning, Herr Lohse.' But we knew the guys as Peter and Roger and they had probably known each other for years serving on the same squadron and unit.

The allocation of flying slots was incredibly rigid and if you missed your time to fly because of weather or aircraft unsuitability then you simply lost your flight for the day and your time was your own. Well, we Air Force types had never known anything like this. If the weather was bad we would find something else to do involving ground duties. To have taken the day off would never have happened – it was unheard of.

There were three squadrons at Cottesmore. A, B and C. B was the British Squadron, A was the Germans and C the Italians. I'm not really sure what that meant because on my course we had British, German and Italian staff and instructors.

When we first started our conversion course to Tornados in the late autumn of 1983 our allocation of flying slots was incredibly early in the morning. We had to report for briefing at something like 3.30a.m. ready to start flying at about 5.15a.m. Inevitably the weather was often very poor at that time in the morning with fog and mist or driving rain, so it wasn't unusual to be stacked – the

term for being released from duty for the rest of the day
– at 4a.m.

One particular day we all went round to the deputy
squadron commander's house, Porky Richardson, and
demanded egg and bacon from his long-suffering wife.
There were about six or seven of us but eggie bakes were
provided for all and we tucked into a hearty breakfast.
Soon enough that morning the beer was out and the
lamp was swinging furiously as we launched into tales
of derring-do from our past flying days.

Most of the German and Italian guys had flown the
F104 Star Fighter previously. The Star Fighter was known
as the Widow maker for a very good reason. It killed lots
of fighter pilots because it was only a single-engine aircraft
and notoriously complex to operate. The Canadians had
also lost a lot of their pilots to the F104 for the very same
reasons. It really was the femme fatale of the fighter world;
if you could keep control of her then apparently she was
a darling to fly. But if you lost concentration for no more
than a few seconds she would unleash a merciless attack
on her hapless pilot. She was also a single seater and the
German pilots in particular really did find it quite difficult
to adapt to flying with a navigator in the back seat.

The RAF pilots and navigators had mostly come from
the cream of the Royal Air Force. Many instructors and as
many ex-Harrier and Lightning pilots were recruited and
the navigators from the Phantom and Buccaneer crews. At
the time the Tornado was still in its infancy as a fighter
jet but it was going to be the spearhead of NATO well
into the twenty-first century.

On that morning I listened to tales from flight commanders and some of the most experienced fighter pilots
in that day's Air Force and I wasn't terribly sure what an

ex-helicopter mate had to offer. I think I was a source of amusement to the rest of the crews. They talked about nothing on the clock but the maker's name in Arabic as they told tales of near misses and extraordinary feats of flying at tens of thousands of feet and at thousands of miles an hour. I'd spent the last eight years plodding through the sky at rarely more than 100mph. But I still had my stories to tell, not least about my collision in the Hawk at Chivenor. I had my Martin-Baker tie presented to me by the company who manufactured my ejection seat which functioned perfectly on the 29 of July 1983.

Anyway the air got hotter and the stories taller as we got drunker. Typical of these occasions, you start off sitting on the sofa but inevitably begin that slide towards the carpet. Still in Porky's house we were absolutely pie-eyed. His wife had cleared up the breakfast plates and just left us to it. Just as I was about to nod off finally Porky's two young children came into the room. It was only 8.30a.m. and they were off to school.

There were many days like that when we just kicked our heels. Flying was off and we would be left to find some other form of entertainment. Stumpy Stoner, my closest friend on the course, had a first-rate pedigree to his name. He was an ex-Lightning pilot, a flying instructor and had flown for three years with the Red Arrows. You couldn't ask for much more than that. Stumpy lived in the mess while his wife and children stayed in their own cottage in Tetbury, Gloucestershire.

Stumpy had a computer – a Commodore 32 – which in those days was quite a special piece of kit. He had a computer game which basically involved trying to wipe out Dracula from the screen. It was an adventure game that gave the player a series of tasks to complete. To start with there were just one or two of us playing but the numbers slowly increased until most people on the station were participating.

The solution to the puzzle became almost an obsession. We would get to a particular obstacle on the screen and the telephones would be red hot as we tried to glean information from others, who were probably carrying out their duties elsewhere on the station. We were very close to overcoming the final hurdle but couldn't work out how to get through a locked door. There was a notice pinned to the door and we had spent days and days trying to open the thing. The notice gave absolutely no information at all, it seemed hopeless. But then one lovely flying day when Stumpy was already airborne it came to him in a flash. He told the air traffic controller on the radio to get an urgent message through to the squadron. We were to use the pin holding up the notice to unlock the door. It worked, we were through with the touch of a keyboard button. Game over. The approach controller made a subsequent transmission to all Cottesmore aircraft announcing that Dracula was dead. By the time we had finished that game even the station commander was as involved in its complexities as the rest of us.

Training on the Tornado before finally taking my place as a fully fledged fighter bomber pilot on the squadron involved the successful completion of two courses. The first at Cottesmore required no more of us than the ability to fly the aeroplane with a rudimentary grasp of its weapon systems. The course lasted four months before moving on to RAF Honington in Suffolk. The courses were vastly different. The Cottesmore course had to be one of the easiest I had ever completed. The Honington course was probably the hardest. RAF Honington was purely a British establishment and it was back to the real Air Force with a very large bump.

By the end of January 1984, I was out of Cottesmore and working my backside off at Honington. Sheila and our two children stayed in our quarter back in Rutland and I became a bachelor during a week in the officer's mess and commuted home every weekend to become a dad again. I don't think I was much of a dad during those four hectic months. There only ever seemed to be enough time to either work or sleep.

The 28 April 1984 was to become quite a memorable day, particularly for Stumpy. By this stage we were flying in formations of four aircraft and using the weapons systems to the full. We were getting more and more used to navigators in their new role beside us as executives. Stumpy had been a single-seat man all his flying career and was finding it extremely difficult to adapt to having someone else in the aircraft with him.

On this particular day Stumpy's backseater was a staff navigator whose role on this sortie was to assess our competence to operate in tactical formation. When we got back for the debrief I was told that my formation flying had been especially good while Stumpy's was well below the required standard and he would have to fly the sortie again. Stumpy hit the roof. He was apoplectic with rage and indignation. He ranted, 'How on earth could a fucking navigator tell me how to fly formation? I did three years on the world's finest formation team, what the hell would talking ballast in the back seat know about formations?'

He was inconsolable and refused to fly with the man ever again. Some ten years later both officers hold the same very senior rank yet refuse to acknowledge each other's existence. They despise each other.

On 8 May 1984 I flew my last training sortie in the Tornado before joining 16 Squadron at RAF Laarbruch, close to the Dutch border in Western Germany. Stan Bowles was my navigator during our training at Honington. He was a young first tourist who was obviously being groomed for higher things. There were occasions when Stan and I rolled across the apron with our hands at each other's throats, each blaming the other for whatever cock-up had occurred during the sortie. We were both incredibly keen to do well and I think overall we did bring out the best in each other. Then we were posted to different squadrons at Laarbruch but we kept up a rapport and a warm affection for each other. Stan was killed during the intense training build-up to the Gulf War. He was one of three air crew killed in a mid-air collision between two Tornados off the coast of East Anglia in the late summer of 1990. Our training was so exacting that I could not even be relieved from my duties for even half a day. Stan was buried by his family but I could not be there to pay my last respects.

I drove over to Germany with Stumpy in his car. My posting was initially to 20 Squadron with him but that was changed at the very last minute. It didn't really matter to me, I was on the threshold of a dream. There were four squadrons based at RAF Laarbruch – 2, 15, 16 and 20. Two Squadron was equipped with the single-seat Jaguar and operated in a reconnaissance role. Fifteen Squadron was the first RAF Tornado Squadron in Germany and 16 Squadron was the second. Both had re-equipped from the Buccaneer. The Buccaneer was deemed to be well past its sell-by date, however, nearly seven years later it was destined to go to war yet again to operate alongside us in our laser-guided bombing attacks on Iraq.

Stumpy and I had chosen the luxurious route to Germany; we would take the overnight ferry from Hull to Rotterdam and had booked a first class cabin. We had obviously come to rely very heavily on our navigators. Stumpy's Ford Sierra estate was chocabloc full with our kit, we even had our bicycles, but not a map between us. This we realised when we landed in Rotterdam. Driving to Hull had not posed too many problems but charting our journey across Holland was a different matter. In fact we arrived in Laarbruch on a Sunday afternoon in good time.

Stumpy's attitude to life was very similar to mine. We both enjoyed adventure and embarked on one only the second week after we had arrived in Germany. The initial pace of squadron life was very laid back. Everything was new to all of us and there was plenty of time to acclimatise. It was a bit like the lull before the storm and the pace was destined to hot up so we took advantage of those early days of leisure. So we bundled both bikes into the back of Stumpy's car and made the three-hour drive south to the River Mosel. We were going to enjoy a weekend's cycling and wine tasting.

We quickly found a Gasthof and booked ourselves in for the weekend in a sleepy little town called Cochem. Stumpy's German was passable but mine was non-existent. The weather was blistering hot, it was just gorgeous. We cycled through the vineyards stopping at farmhouses and wine kellars along the route to sample the local wines. We cycled and we drank then we drank some more before wobbling on our way.

Saturday rolled into Sunday and we decided to stop for Sunday lunch before a final cycle ride back to the car to make our way back to Laarbruch. While we were obviously tourists we had done our best to avoid the obvious bars and restaurants frequented by most Brits abroad. We wanted to enjoy Germany like the natives did and dip into their way of life. We found a little restaurant that I would have cycled straight past, it was so hidden and discreet. Stumpy had served a tour on the Lightning at RAF Guttersloh and his memories of those days were coming back and paying dividends during our weekend jaunt. I popped my head around the door of the restaurant to be pleasantly surprised. Half a dozen or so crisp white tablecloths, dark and heavy oak furniture and everything spotlessly clean. The menu didn't make much sense to me but Stumpy guided us both through it. I settled for a veal steak and chips washed down with yet more local wine.

The hausfrau who served us our food was all that you could imagine of a German waitress. She wore a very colourful national-style dress, straining over her enormous chest but she also wore a very jolly smile. Four stones lighter and she would have been a very attractive lady but here she was, a little on the wrong side of forty and showing all the effects of a life of very serious eating and drinking. We finished a delightful meal and asked for the bill but all we got was more of her beaming smile and two glasses of a clear liquid she told us was schnapps. It was pure firewater. She gestured to us to drink saying that the drink was 'Frei', it was on the house, and she wasn't going to leave us alone until we had emptied our glasses. In typical fighter pilot tradition we touched glasses, toasted our charming hostess and threw the lot down in one. Seconds later two more glasses of schnapps arrived. Our hostess's intentions were becoming clearer by the minute. She had taken a shine to both of us and

I don't know whether she wanted to disappear out the back with one at a time or both at once!

The effects of the wine and the meal and then the schnapps were beginning to show and I think both Stumpy and I felt warm and somnolent. We were very pleasantly pickled. All of a sudden the hausfrau's heaving breasts seemed like a very comfortable pillow on which to rest our weary heads. We finished the second glass of schnapps a little slower than the first while pleading for the bill. It was more sensible to settle our account and cycle off. But she was having none of it and more schnapps arrived. She wanted our bodies and was not going to part with them without a struggle. I think it was Stumpy who threw a 50 mark note down on the table which would have more than covered the cost of our meal and wine and we both dived for the door, jumped on our bikes and cycled away like demons. I think she would have eaten us a alive, quite a scary thought.

Back to our training in the fast lane and the speed very definitely began to hot up as each day passed.

Initially we were very restricted on what we could do with the Tornado. For instance, we couldn't fire the guns as they hadn't yet been released to service. There were some quite severe restrictions on operating speeds but for the moment all of this suited me down to the ground. I was finding it enough of a challenge just keeping up with the aircraft limitations they had allowed us. And I had the next year or so to grow with the aeroplane. As I became more proficient I was allowed to move on to some new and more exacting task. How on earth the youngsters coped with the aircraft years later when they had to learn everything straightaway I shall never know. We were dealing with a brand-new aeroplane and our expertise evolved with its development. As the years went on, the Tornado reached maturity with every one of its complex systems to be tackled all at once.

I'm not sure whether or not the Air Force made a mistake in sending its very best fast jet pilots on to the Tornado force, particularly the flight commanders. Seeing those senior officers at the end of the day relaxing over a cold beer it was like a hall of fame of the fast jet world. On their previous squadrons each one of them would have been a guiding light to the rest but now they were just another name. Previously these men were top dogs, now they were just one among many in those early and exciting days. They were reduced to the same level and they didn't like it. Like the rest of us they had to learn the ropes all over again. The back-biting on the squadron among the flight commanders was fierce. I have to say it did not encourage a strong feeling of camaraderie or support for one's fellow men. Their presence at times created bad feeling and resentment among the rest of us.

I closed my eyes and ears to a lot of what was going on and concentrated on being just as good as I could at my job. There was good and bad about being where I was during that time. I was on a squadron alongside some of the very best pilots and navigators in the RAF. This made them the best in the world and at this stage I hadn't developed the supreme arrogance as a fast jet operator. I was still practising my lines. I could already drink to world-class standard but I was still learning the banter that goes with the territory.

Rod Sergeant had this irritating habit of calling everyone 'dear boy' from the station commander down. He considered that navigators were beneath contempt and ought to have been replaced by an extra fuel tank. The young navs on the squadron were terrified of flying with him, he could hardly bring himself to be civil to them and his demands on their skills were so exacting that they could never hope to reach the standards he set. It wasn't unusual to see a grown man in tears walking back disconsolately from the aircraft having just flown a sortie with the dreaded Sergeant. He was an arrogant sod but he was also one of many. And what a pilot. Sergeant could make the aeroplane sing, he had total and absolute control of that machine. I am reluctant to admit this but back then he was already twice the pilot that I will ever be.

Simon Tomkins was the officer commanding A flight, my flight commander. He had a very slow and measured manner about him. He knew the aeroplane's technical systems inside out, in fact the manufacturers even took his advice on changing some of the finer detail of the designs. On the ground he was a real plodder and in many ways didn't inspire anyone's imagination as to what a fighter pilot would be like. But in the air he was a different man. Most of us seemed to leave half of our brains behind as soon as we left terra firma, but he just became a tiger. The difference was profound. While many of us would struggle to keep up with the aircraft, he just seemed to be entirely in his element, like a heavy sealion which out of water is a helpless, almost pitiful creature but in the water is transformed into the graceful master of his own element.

Flying from a German base was the real thing for all of us. We were ten minutes' flying time away from the East/West Germany border and two aircraft and their crews were on permanent fifteen-minute standby to launch an attack on designated targets within Warsaw Pact countries. They were armed with nuclear

225

weapons possessing sufficient power to have made the bombing of Hiroshima and Nagasaki seem like lighting a match next to a blazing furnace.

The aircraft were housed in a cordoned-off area known as QRA – quick reaction alert – and a number of crews would live in the 'Q' shed for twenty-four hours at a time. We had our own dormitory, kitchen and chef and were always fully kitted out and ready to react to the first sound of the klaxon. Many of the crews even slept in their full flying kit – I didn't. We were regularly checked for our ability to get to the aircraft in time and from the moment the warning sounded the stopwatch was on us. We sprinted across the apron into our hardened aircraft shelter and then up the steps to the aircraft to switch on the battery master and check in on the secure direct communications link to operations.

We checked in using a secret code word, a combination of letters and numbers that regularly changed and made no sense to anyone else. The watch would stop and we were informed of the time at a later stage. We were normally well inside a couple of minutes. The first words that we would hear from the controller as we checked in were always: 'Practice, practice, practice', informing us that this was just a drill.

Whenever we heard the klaxon sound we acted as though it was all for real and that within the next half an hour or so some poor Russian establishment would be obliterated and the whole world on its way to Armageddon. We were required to know our target details and the method of attack to the letter. We were regularly quizzed by our mission planners and there was only ever one pass mark and that was 100 per cent.

The last communication we would have had with base

before starting engines and rolling forward was confirmation of a codeword. We would then ignore all else for fear of being spoofed by our enemies. We never knew for sure but we always suspected and it was subsequently proven that there was one final link in the chain. If we had been launched to carry out a nuclear attack there was no system of recall. If the politicians decided at the very last second to stand down then two RAF fighters were to be scrambled to shoot us down before we had armed our buckets of sunshine.

On one particular day in July 1985 I was standing in 'Q' with Phil Duncan, a close friend and one of the best navigators I have ever flown with. The klaxon sounded and we rushed to the aircraft and I checked in on the closed radio just as Phil joined me on the intercom. Sue, the mission controller, replied with the release codeword. There was no mention of practice. I nearly crapped myself and Phil was physically sick. Within seconds Sue was desperately trying to correct her grievous mistake. She was screaming across the interphone 'Pablo, this is a practice!'

But by the letter of the law I had been released on my deadly mission, I was to ignore all other transmissions. I pushed the starter button for the right engine at about the same time as a burly Royal Air Force police corporal climbed the ladders still fastened to the side of the aircraft, put a machine gun to my head and said: 'If you don't shut it down, Sir, I am going to spread your fucking brains all over this hangar.'

There were all sorts of feelings running through my head; fear and the sure knowledge that I would be dead within the hour, no matter what. Everything went into slow motion as though none of it was happening for real.

Within a minute the head of operations was at the side of the aircraft. Phil and I realised that there had been an error and it was a practice.

With enormous relief we shut down our aeroplane and were replaced by another crew.

I think it took me days to wind down from that experience. For those few seconds which had seemed like hours, I actually believed that I was going to be one of the very first elements in the start of World War Three. Long before the collapse of the Warsaw Pact and the reunification of Germany, QRA was scrapped very discreetly, to the relief of all of us. It had been like sitting on a time bomb and for those few moments in time someone had accidentally lit the fuse.

RAF Laarbruch had been built shortly after the end of the Second World War, and rumour had it that the man responsible for the construction had been subsequently jailed. The plans had been drawn in metres and he was alleged to have shaved a bit of everything to build the base in yards and thus pocketing the difference. It did show in that many rooms just felt slightly too small and the perimeter roads were not quite wide enough.

Laarbruch formed a vital part of the front line of Nato's defences. There were no frills, everything about the base showed that the station was on permanent standby and ready to go to war at a moment's notice. Back in the UK there was still a hint of spit and polish about most RAF stations but not at Laarbruch. Instead of alternately painted black and white kerbstones everything was drab green. Trees were planted everywhere to try to break up the outline of a military airfield. It was quite successful, the base was hard enough for us to find from the air or road and we lived there.

At the end of each runway was a massive pile of stone chippings and a number of bulldozers covered in inhibiting grease and tarpaulin. The chippings would be used to fill holes in the runway caused by enemy bombs, and the engines of the bulldozers were run up daily and kept in fine tune. There were countless exercises either calling a single squadron to readiness or involving the entire station. There were also regular call-outs from home invariably in the middle of the night and initiated by Land Rovers driving past our houses with lights flashing and horns and klaxons blaring. The local Germans loved us! We'd report for duty and then tuck into bacon sandwiches in our operations rooms.

All of the ops and aircraft were tucked safely behind several feet of reinforced concrete. Often during the early stages of these exercises we could be kept guessing for hours on end. Was this an exercise or the real thing? Of course it was always an exercise but who was to say at the time whether or not we were poised to engage in the real thing?

Sheila and the kids joined me at Laarbruch about six weeks after Stumpy and I had escaped the clutches of the rampant German frau in the Mosel. I had bought my dream car – a metallic grey BMW 525i – and I drove back over to England to collect my family. We had been allocated a married quarter on the outskirts of the town of Goch just twelve miles north of the airfield itself. Initially we hated it. Until now our married quarter had always been on base or very close to it. The thought of having to commute for an hour each day was nothing short of depressing.

As a result of an incident that happened within the first few days of arriving at Laarbruch, I was determined to learn to speak German just as soon as I possibly could. Knowing the language would also help me to enjoy as much as I could of the culture and the way of life in my temporary country of residence. A group of us out on an evening drive eventually wound up at a riverside gelateria – an ice cream shop – near Arnhem on the banks of the River Rhine just inside the German border. The senior member of our group had only recently completed several years in Germany, so I naturally assumed that he would be our linguist for the day.

When the waiter arrived to take our order not one word in German was exchanged, and I was embarrassed by the conduct of my friends. They held a typically British attitude: if he can't understand what you are saying in English then just repeat it in a louder voice. I was trying to apologise to the young German man but the more I apologised the less he appeared to understand.

A few days later I returned to that ice-cream parlour to seek him out with my phrase book in hand and a couple of phonetically prepared sentences written down. One of the first things I did with Sheila and the children was to take them to an ice-cream parlour where I ordered *Erdbeereis* – strawberry ice cream – and when Eleanor insisted she wanted raspberry flavour I ordered *Himbeereis* instead. My children were highly impressed by my grasp of the German language. Little did they know that those words were the sum total of my vocabulary at that stage. By the time we left Germany in the summer of 1991, I could hold a reasonable conversation in German on almost any subject. It never ceased to astonish me the number of servicemen and their families who spent many years in Germany and never even bothered to learn the simple courtesies of *bitte* or *danke schön*.

During our off-duty time as a family we travelled extensively throughout Europe. I still love the order and discipline that permeates the well-organised German nation. I look back at Margaret Thatcher's prediction that the reunification of Germany would take several years when in fact it took as many months, even if there is still much of the divisive curtain to iron out.

Life in Germany for us remained very much a Monday to Friday affair, but the working day got longer and longer. From that blissful summer of 1984 to the onset of winter, nine to five became six-thirty to eight-thirty and that meant a fourteen-hour working day. I would see my children to bed on a Sunday evening and I may not see them awake again until the following Saturday morning.

Even today, when the RAF has no recognisable enemy, the Warsaw Pact is defunct and Germany is reunited, guys are still working their arses off for no good reason. Marriages have suffered, including my own. At the end of a hard working week it was great to unwind at happy hour in the bar on Friday evening. But this was no consolation to a long-suffering wife who had dutifully ministered to the needs of a hubby who arrived home every evening only to go straight to bed and was on his way to work before she stirred the next morning. Wasting half of Saturday sleeping off the excesses of the previous night did not normally make for a cordial relationship either.

In those days I was lucky enough to have an iron constitution. I could crawl home from the bar in the early hours of Saturday morning having drunk most of my buddies under the table and be ready to play with my children after no more than a couple of hours sleep.

Wives felt neglected and in the extreme sought comfort elsewhere. Sometimes those new liaisons ended a marriage for good, in other cases they just destroyed the individuals concerned to no end result. It's strange how, after the Gulf War, men who had sustained a marriage that had long since died, vowed to cut the ties and seek a new life for themselves. Some very senior officers involved in the Gulf did just that and divorces followed by new marriages were announced soon after it was all over. One squadron commander abandoned his own wife and children and set up home with the wife of one of the other squadron commanders. It doesn't seem to have done his career any harm. At the moment he commands a front-line fighter station in East Anglia. We were an attractive bunch of guys. Getting women into bed for anyone with such a high profile was no problem and it became for some no more than an amusing pastime.

A regular squadron detachment was to the Italian Air Force base of Decimomannu in southern Sardinia. The island is idyllic and the reason for us being there was because of its incredibly good weather, the sun always shone and we could get on with our flying. The RAF base itself was an absolute shithole; the accommodation was appalling, the food a disgrace and if it wasn't for the weather it would have driven us mad within days. But we were there to fly and the conditions were always superb.

The purpose of the detachment was to reach the ACE standard in weaponry. Allied Forces Central Europe set a list of requirements to be met by us in various weaponry skills. We needed to get our bombs off within a few feet of the target by dive bombing, level bombing and loft bombing. Strafing was one of the most demanding skills to develop but such was the accuracy and harmony of the 27mm Mauser cannons fitted to the Tornado that we always exceeded the required standards many fold. All of the targets were situated on a piece of headland known as Frasca Range and about fifteen minutes' flying time from Deci.

Our ground crews enjoyed the element of competition almost as much as we did. The allowed time to refuel and re-arm a Tornado was in the order of one and a half hours. A good crew could turn a jet around inside twenty minutes.

The Italian air traffic and range controllers could not disguise their heavy Latin accents, although their grasp of the English language was first rate. The international language of aviation is English and we are merely lucky that it is our mother tongue. But the Italians coped admirably except their English was heavily doctored by that unique Italian accent.

We air crews loved it and never lost a chance to speak on the radio, copying the Italian voices on the ground. A controller would call over the radio, and before we were clear to take off we would have to confirm that the canopy was 'clos-ed and lock-ed'. This we would do mimicking their accents.

It was hilarious for us but they had the last laugh. Following our confirmation that the canopy was indeed 'clos-ed and lock-ed' we were instructed to sit in the blazing sun for a further ten minutes until cleared for takeoff. A voice would come over on the radio: 'Now, you say to me, "I sit here in the blazing sun for ten minutes".' No amount of apologising or retracting our mickey-taking would do. The voice would only confirm: 'Is no good, you'ave another nine an' a'alf minute to go.'

Once I was sitting on the pan at Deci ready to take off and return to Laarbruch having lost my trusty service dress cap on a evening trip off the base. The cap had been with me for years; most officers' hats are their trade mark and mine bore the beer and oil and sweat stains marking years of sterling service. I was very sad to have lost it and had given up all hope of ever seeing my old hat again. But then over the airwaves a voice crackled: 'Ay! Wha' is you name? Does one o' you guys lost a' at? We foun' 'im in a taxi an' we don' wan' 'im, he smell anyways.' Once again the Italians had come up trumps because the name clearly marked inside the hat was P.J.D. Mason, it was mine and I was happy to taxi back onto the stand to claim it.

On 1 July 1988, I was promoted from flight lieutenant to squadron leader and posted to XV Squadron as training officer. The move was going to take me just half a mile to the other side of the airfield but it was to move me a million miles from where I really wanted to be. I had nothing against XV Squadron or the men I served with there. But as soon as I accepted my promotion I realised what a desperate mistake it was to be.

I loved flying and my experiences on fast jets will always be like a dream come true. But I am no executive and began to hate and despise everything my new position stood for. There were lots of perks to being a squadron leader. On a station the size of Laarbruch I was among the thirty or so most senior officers of a total compliment of around 4,000 officers and men. So a simple request for an item of clothing from Supply Squadron would normally be met by a swift and positive result.

Sheila also noticed an incredible difference. She was now wife of Squadron Leader Mason. We had our parking slot both at the squadron and outside the officers' mess.

What I really hated about myself was the fact that I

quickly became just like many of the other squadron leaders – a pompous oaf. For years I'd vowed that if ever I was promoted things would be different. My greatest loyalty would be to those who worked for me and not those I was trying to impress. As it turned out I became like all the rest.

9

Reflections

I shall never forget the afternoon in May 1994 when I nervously called up a friend on her mobile phone to give her the awesome news I had only just received minutes earlier. She had just turned into the drive of her home near Saffron Walden in Essex and she turned off the car's engine to hear what I had to say, knowing neither she nor I could wait for her to call me on a clearer land line inside the house.

There was no time to spare, the whole world or at least everyone I knew had to know. That afternoon as I wondered for the millionth time if I would ever fly for a living again my prayers were answered.

The whole sequence of events took place within the space of twenty-four hours. It was Tuesday afternoon of that momentous week when the business telephone at our pet shop in Peterborough rang. I was stacking shelves with pet food and doggy paraphernalia when a female voice at the other end of the phone asked to speak to Paul James David Mason. Very few people know me as Paul, the name I was christened with. My nickname, Pablo, came from my very early days as a young trainee officer when I joined the RAF sporting a Zapata moustache.

I cautiously asked the caller what it was in connection

with and she introduced herself as Louise Blackburn, assistant to the director of operations at Airtours International. Would I be available for interview and possibly employment?

I went into fluent Araldite, speaking in pure wallpaper paste. It was just so exciting and a huge surprise so totally out of the blue. Of course Airtours was one of a dozen airlines I had written to inquiring about a job and one of the few that had bothered to write a personal reply, even if the answer was that: they were unlikely to need fresh pilots for at least another year but my name would be kept on file because I had the level of skills that they could make use of in the future, were I still available. Things had obviously changed very quickly over the few days since I had received that letter.

Louise continued, 'Could you attend an interview at 9a.m. tomorrow morning at our Manchester headquarters?' She added that I would be required to start almost immediately. I didn't like to sound too keen but the truth is that I would have been willing to walk to Manchester on my hands for that interview.

Not one of my suits fitted. For much of the two years since leaving the Air Force I had sunk into deep despair. I think part of the compensation had been to eat for comfort and the net result was that I had piled on three stones. I was an extremely fat bastard and my suits barely fitted where they touched. Here I was at almost 5p.m. and I had nothing to wear. I jumped into a taxi into Peterborough town centre to the John Lewis store just as they were closing the shutters. But I was a desperate man and I already had my hand through the door. That store would not be closing until I had bought myself a new suit and a pair of smart shoes.

With suit and shoes in hand the next stop was the local library to find out all I could about Airtours and the aeroplanes it flew. Right into the small hours I read about the McDonald Douglas MD83, a twin-engined airliner which carried 173 passengers. Half an hour before I had never heard of the thing but now I could have sat an A'level in it. Back issues of *Flight International* gave me the basic structure of the company and the various types and numbers of aircraft that it operates, and of course the names of all the senior directors. I burned the midnight oil and crammed as much information into my thick head as I could that I thought I may be asked at interview. That left me only a couple of hours to sleep before I needed to get into the car and drive up to Manchester. I wasn't tired anyway, I was too excited to sleep. I didn't even wear my suit for the car journey, I laid it over the back seat of the car and changed in the lavatory at Airtours' reception.

The chief pilot and his fleet captain conducted the interview. I thought things went reasonably well but they kept giving me information about the company rather than quizzing about my own credentials. It seemed much of the previous night's swotting had all been rather academic.

Towards the end of the interview the chief pilot obviously assumed that I was in the position of considering several offers from other airlines. He wanted to know that if he offered me a flying job would I accept and could I start soon? I didn't realise then he had in mind the very next morning. Well, had he suggested that very evening it would have been fine by me.

By the time I got home I was completely knackered having hardly slept at all for the best part of forty-eight hours. I flaked out on the bed still wearing my suit only to be woken by Lisa, my partner, an hour later at 3p.m.

that same day to be told I had got the job. I was to be a first officer on an aeroplane I had only just heard about a few hours before. I had got the job and was expected to start work at 9 o'clock the very next morning.

I'd started working for my civilian licences before leaving the RAF on 14 November 1991. But those early studies had been interrupted by the Gulf War. Just before I flew out to the Middle East in December 1990, I had received the results of my first exams and to my extreme satisfaction I gained a first time pass in all subjects. The course had been by correspondence for almost a year with regular assessments from my postal tutor in Bournemouth. The last three weeks prior to the exam were spent in a crammer at the same aviation academy there.

I was on standby to deploy to the Gulf and was warned that I could be pulled out of the classroom at any moment. I don't think I have worked any harder than I did during that time. I was leaving the RAF and was determined to continue my flying career as an airline pilot. Little did I know then that it would take me a further three years to gain my Air Transport Pilot's Licence and the best part of £10,000 to do it. One of the conditions of gaining a commercial licence is that all of the examinations must be passed within a twelve-month period. Five months in the Gulf followed by a crash in an RAF Tornado wiped out the best part of that.

I wrote to the Civil Aviation Authority asking for more time to complete my studies. After an initial refusal my situation was treated with a good deal of compassion and I was given another twelve months to obtain a commercial licence. I still had further exams to take but gaining that ticket meant I was almost home and dry. But there were many times during the four years after I quit the RAF that I honestly believed I would never fly for a living again.

When I left the Air Force on 14 November 1991, I felt totally abandoned by the service to which I had loyally dedicated most of the last eighteen years. I bought a house in Oakham, Rutland, about six miles from Cottesmore from where I had embarked upon my fast jet career on the Tornado and where I was to spend the last three months of my RAF career.

They were not good months. I had returned from the Gulf to be treated like a celebrity by the public at large and like a leper and charlatan by the Air Force and many of my former colleagues. The future for myself and for my family was uncertain. After a two-minute interview with the station commander I walked out of the main gates shortly after midday never giving a backward glance and continued on my way the six miles to the home I had bought for Sheila and our children.

By 1 December 1991 I was no longer a resident at that address having moved to a little three-bed semi near Basingstoke in Hampshire that Sheila and I had bought as a nest egg eleven years previously. We'd only ever lived in it together for a total of four days, but I was to stay there until the following August. That insignificant little box of a house was to be my hideaway, a place where I could reconsider my life and come to terms with so much that had now gone forever.

I wasn't alone for very long. Lisa and I have now been together for nearly four years and that is the way it is. I don't really want to say very much about us, not just because our relationship is private, but I also believe Sheila and the children deserve to be spared a public scrutiny of all our lives.

241

I think that the Air Force for all its stuffy image really does care for its own. During much of the three months prior to actually leaving the service I had gone on various resettlement courses and seminars. Some of these I had organised for myself but they were mostly at the Joint Services Resettlement Centre at Catterick in Yorkshire. I had a vague inkling to start up my own business and looked at many opportunities from takeaway pizza franchises to selling mobile telephones. I had to try something because as I left the RAF the world of commercial aviation was as flat as a pancake in the wake of the Gulf War. As I saw it I was unlikely to secure a place on the flight deck for at least a couple of years.

The resettlement courses were staffed by very well meaning and capable retired servicemen. They were all thoroughly nice blokes but despite all the resettlement training and my total conviction that I was a man of the world and there were few surprises left, I was soon to realise what absolute animals some members of the human race really are. Within a couple of months of leaving the Air Force I had been relieved of £10,000 of my hard-earned savings by someone I thought was one of my closest friends. He and a business colleague had a fantastic money-making scheme which 'couldn't possibly fail'. Three years down the road I am still waiting for my pot of gold but I've given up chasing rainbows.

I still think most of my fellow men are good people but the percentage of bastards outside the military circle is far greater than the ones inside. Just two years after the end of the Gulf War and a year after I had agonised and wrestled with my own story, *Pablo's War*, I was in for another disappointment. A journalist I had met and shared confidences with out in the Gulf was about to try and stitch me up good and proper. He knew everything about my personal life and my relationship with my wife, Sheila, and he knew about Lisa too. I had confided in him as a friend and he knew everything about me right from the very start. Men talk like that together especially when the heat is on and no one is sure if they will have a future at all.

This man, his name is irrelevant, told me all about himself too in fairly candid terms. I would never betray his confidence but he has betrayed mine. In the end his story in a Sunday newspaper was fairly feeble. It was about how I had left my wife and children and had set up home with another woman. None of this I would deny, but I am sorry that he called time on our friendship for the sake of a few forgettable lines that were destined to be the next day's fish and chip wrapping.

Lisa and I moved from our little house after it was sold. The entire proceeds of the sale were handed over to Sheila and the children. At the time I didn't want the bother of dealing with material possessions, so we rented another little box down the road and moved our few belongings into it. It was another hiding hole for me and I think for Lisa too.

There was the occasional foray into London. After writing my first book I was invited to give a number of TV and radio interviews. Wherever a military aircraft was involved in a news story I was usually asked if I could offer some expert advice, especially if the aircraft was a Tornado. It put a little bit of excitement into life but it also made me feel incredibly vulnerable.

I had earned a reputation among my colleagues for having a skin as thick as a rhinoceros. But now I was getting to the stage where my body and mind just couldn't take much more. They say that leaving your family, losing your job and moving house are three of the most traumatic events that can affect a person's life. I can tell you that is absolutely true. Within the space of a few months, having just returned from war, I had nearly killed myself and a dear friend in an aircraft crash, given up my job, left my wife and children and moved house three times.

It wasn't long before I was to seek psychiatric help. Sheila and I have tried to stay on friendly terms and during those early months of 1992 she was desperately concerned for my well-being and believed that I wasn't far from trying to end it all. And she wasn't very far from the truth. How ironic that when she persuaded me to turn to the RAF and I then sought psychiatric help at RAF Wroughton, I discovered a close friend and Gulf War comrade had already attempted to take his own life.

It wasn't long before I found out about several other of those Gulf War heroes who had sought the help of the trick cyclists at Wroughton to sort out the mess their lives had become. I spent several sessions with the head of psychiatry, Wing Commander Gordon Turnbull, a world-renowned expert in the field of post traumatic stress disorder. I enjoyed my visits but within a couple of months decided that they weren't much help and that I'd got to sort out my own problems.

At one stage during those dark days I walked with a large bottle of paracetamol in my pocket and frequently sat alone on railway bridges. But now I am firmly convinced that the world has got to put up with me for at least another thirty years. I looked around and suddenly I saw a chink of light at the end of a very long and dark tunnel. Life really is worth living. I should stop being a turkey and if life wasn't going to come and grab me then I should go and grab it.

Lisa and I walked and talked for ages or rather I talked and she just listened. I reasoned that the best place to get a flying job would be somewhere in the Far East on the Pacific Rim. One or two Japanese airlines were recruiting and I was almost ready to hop on board a long-distance flight and knock on a few doors. Unfortunately that was about the time that the Pacific Rim joined the rest of the world in its recession. I had to think again. I sat at home and felt sorry for myself, so there was no change there.

Lisa got a job as a receptionist for a local skip hire company. At least it gave us a small income and something different to talk about. Regularly we bought *Dalton's Weekly*, a newspaper which advertises businesses for sale. I still had a few pounds in the bank to my name but as Mr Micawber warned against, expenditure was definitely exceeding income.

As we scoured the pages of *Dalton's* we spotted a pet food shop in Peterborough that was up for sale and seemed reasonably priced. In fact it was so cheap we could almost afford it. We arranged an appointment to visit. The place was an absolute tip, a shambles of empty shelves and rotting food. Deep freezers in the back had been switched off, full of tripe and offal, for almost two years. Even the rats I discovered lying there among the putrefaction had given up the ghost and died.

We decided that we had to buy the shop, dreadful and unpromising as it was. We had both spotted a ray of hope. We never spoke during the whole visit but somehow both Lisa and I knew that this place would either make us or break us. The place had been run by a mother and daughter who had obviously lost interest in both the business and themselves. I made a ridiculous cash offer for the shop and it was almost immediately accepted. On 14 May 1993 at exactly 9a.m. the shop became ours. The whole transaction was completed within little more than a month.

Lisa enrolled on a four-week course in dog grooming in Stockport, Cheshire. After three weeks I couldn't bear to be alone for a moment longer so I drove almost 200 miles to pick her up and bring her home. We built a little plastic 'oxygen tent' in the bedroom of the one-bed flat above our shop. There we lived as we gradually put together our new life. We scrubbed, bleached, disinfected and polished every single corner of our new business and home. We didn't even allow our closest friends to visit until we had saved up the money to replace the sticky and filth-encrusted carpets of the flat with the cheapest office cord that we could find. As the customers started coming back to the revitalised little shop so my own self-respect and self-esteem also returned.

Within months the newspapers who had plotted my course through the Gulf War had found me out. But I didn't mind, I was proud that the world should know about our little venture in Peterborough. They were kind to me and there were a few stories about the pet shop which at the end of the day was all good for business.

The pet shop is in one of the older parts of the town which has become home to a mixed community. There are Greeks, Italians, Chinese, Indian and some of the older English residents who never moved away. But there is a tremendous community spirit. Within weeks we had been adopted and no member of the press or media who intended us any harm would have got within half a mile of us. It was a lovely place to rebuild our shattered lives and I will never forget that.

I have been flying for Airtours for the best part of a year now and I love every moment of my job. At first some of the passengers recognised my name as the captain and I were announced as the air crew for the flight. Some of them were keen on aviation and had picked up a copy of my book, *Pablo's War*, back at Birmingham airport. Very soon the cabin crew would arrive in the cockpit with one or two copies, asking for me to sign my name inside the cover. I felt nervous about courting publicity when I was so new in the job, and I hated the thought that any of my fellow air crew should ever think I was trading on the past. But now it doesn't matter, people must accept me as I am and I am proud of the many things that I have done.

I am, as ever, proudest of all of my two children. Now they are growing teenagers with minds and opinions of their own and I love them for it. My daughter, Eleanor, is a beautiful and elegant young lady with a brain that puts her father into the shade. And one of the proudest moments I have so far shared with my son, Michael, is the day a couple of years ago when I walked with him as he went along to join the local branch of the Air Cadets. It is his dream to become a pilot in the RAF and I dearly wish that he too achieves that dream. He had wanted me to go along with him for that first meeting but as we got to the door he just said, 'Thanks Dad, see you later' and then he disappeared inside without so much as a backward glance.

That moment took me back some thirty odd years . . .

9

Glossary

bang out
: To use the ejection seat, also known as a Martin Baker let-down. The Martin Baker Company manufactures all RAF ejection seats.

batting
: Cleaning, washing and ironing. In days long gone an officer would be allocated his own Batman, whose sole duty would be as a domestic servant.

brevet
: The uniform 'wings' badge worn over the left breast pocket.

combat ready check
: A test of a pilot's competence to carry out the squadron's role, usually the last major hurdle after 3 or 4 years of flying training.

comms
: Radio communications.

control surfaces
: The moving panels on an aircraft's wings, fin and tailplane which steer it around the skies. The normal control surfaces are ailerons, rudder and elevator.

deployment location
: A discreet landing site a comfortable distance away from recognisable military installations, which would thus afford the aircraft some immunity from surprise attack.

diversion kit
: An overnight bag containing toothbrush, toothpaste, razor etc.

flight location
: The site of the flight commander's tent or command post.

'G' force
: The acceleration force due to gravity, much the same as being pinned to a roller coaster seat during a steep turn.

'G' (pull on)
: To apply positive 'G'. Imagine being pinned to that roller coaster seat as it loops the loop.

jankers
: A punishment detail which usually involved a totally meaningless task like painting coal or cutting grass with scissors.

load factor
: An ever increasing workload, both mental and physical, designed to push each individual close to his limits, sometimes irretrievably beyond.

loadmaster
: The crewmember responsible for the aircraft's load, be it passengers, freight, ammunition or casualties etc.

MINEVAL — A 'mini' evaluation of a squadron's ability to perform its assigned task, normally organised at station level. This would lead on to MAXEVAL and finally TACEVAL which would be organised by Group Headquarters and test the entire station in its duties.

nav-bag — Navigation bag. A grey canvas briefcase containing maps, pens, rulers and all of the necessary flight planning paraphernalia.

OLEO — The main undercarriage leg.

Operational Conversion Unit — A training establishment organised to train and prepare aircrew prior to joining their squadrons.

payload — Load carrying capability measured in pounds or kilograms.

pitch-up manoeuvre — Raising the aircraft's nose to enter a climb.

pylon — The far aft section of the helicopter fuselage, behind the main cabin and containing control cables and some of the radio boxes.

QNH — The atmospheric pressure which would indicate height above sea level when set on the altimeter.

Ranger — A deployment of one or two aircraft, usually overseas and usually over the weekend!

reticle — The crossed wires, circle and aiming mark of a gun or weapons aiming sight.

runway numbers — Runways are numbered with reference to their magnetic heading. For instance, runway 18 would indicate 180 degrees, a heading of south.

Scruffs Bar — A self-service officers bar where both dress regulations and licensing hours were eased considerably. You could relax with a beer after night flying or playing sport, without having to change from smelly clothes into a jacket and tie.

stick (of troops) — A stick of troops would number about eight, normally with a junior non-commissioned officer in charge.

tasking — Carrying out flying tasks and duties as directed by Group Headquarters.

tasking authority — The higher authority responsible for directing flying operations, normally 38 Group Headquarters at RAF Upavon in Wiltshire.

tasking board — A wall-mounted programme of flying tasks arranged in chronological order against a list of aircrew names. Thus we were able to plan our lives a month or so ahead.

theatre conversion — Training in a new or unfamiliar geographical area. In this case, I was very experienced on the Wessex but not in hot and humid Hong Kong.

time expired (parachute) — Outlived its useful service life, the equivalent of being beyond its sell-by date.

wing-over — A semi-aerobatic manoeuvre comprising a steep climb and hard turn into a steep descent.